The Full Circle

A guide to help women find their feet, claim their power and regain their lives

Paulette Archer

The Full Circle: A guide to help women find their feet, claim their power and regain their lives. © Paulette Archer 2018

www.thefullcirclebook.com

The moral rights of Paulette Archer to be identified as the author of this work have been asserted in accordance with the Copyright Act 1968.

First published in Australia 2018 by Gowor International Publishing

www.goworinternationalpublishing.com

ISBN 978-0-9945944-1-9

Any opinions expressed in this work are exclusively those of the author and are not necessarily the views held or endorsed by Gowor International Publishing.

All rights reserved. No part of this publication may be reproduced or transmitted by any means, electronic, photocopying or otherwise, without prior written permission of the author.

Disclaimer
All the information, techniques, skills and concepts contained within this publication are of the nature of general comment only and are not in any way recommended as individual advice. The intent is to offer a variety of information to provide a wider range of choices now and in the future, recognising that we all have widely diverse circumstances and viewpoints. Should any reader choose to make use of the information herein, this is their decision, and the author and publisher/s do not assume any responsibilities whatsoever under any conditions or circumstances. The author does not take responsibility for the business, financial, personal or other success, results or fulfilment upon the readers' decision to use this information. It is recommended that the reader obtain their own independent advice.

Dedicated to the women in this world who want to find their feet, claim their power and regain their lives.

"We are made wise not by the recollection of our past, but by the responsibility for our future."

— Oscar Wilde

A Personal Note from the Publisher

To the reader,

As the Founder of Gowor International Publishing, I make it part of my practice to offer a personal review for my authors about their book. The reason I do this is so that you, as the reader, can glean a further understanding into why this book is about to become a valuable part of your life.

The story of how *The Full Circle* came to be in your hands is one of my favorite stories for the simple reason that it demonstrates how the force of destiny can unexpectedly lead us to great places we never thought we would go. I met Paulette several years ago when she attended one of my live author training programs in Melbourne, Australia. Paulette attended the training to support a friend and so, didn't have a personal intention of writing a book herself.

During the training, I witnessed Paulette's mind opening to the possibility of sharing her story of getting back on her feet after facing divorce as well as a series of other life challenges. By the end of the training, she was on a mission to finish a manuscript and publish the book, and now that mission has come full circle – just like Paulette. This unfolding of events made me know that this book is truly special and that it *is* simply destined to be in your hands.

Paulette inspires me, not only because she follows the inner nudges to tell her story, but because she genuinely cares about the wellbeing of other people – men and women inclusive. Every time I am in Paulette's presence, I feel her strength as a woman and it moves me to become a greater woman myself. She reminds me that we can overcome our challenges no matter how defeating they may feel at the time we encounter them, and that it is our attitude towards our experiences in life that determines the outcome we get.

This book is a reflection of everything that Paulette is – simply magnificent and carefully refined. I know that her teachings will guide you to come full circle so that you can find your feet again amidst adversity, and her words will give you the inspiration you need to do so.

I look forward to hearing how you enjoyed the book.

With inspiration,

Emily Gowor

Founder of Gowor International Publishing

Table of Contents

A Personal Note from the Publisher vii

Table of Contents ix

Preface xi

Introduction: My Circle Begins 1

1: Love, Is There A Better Way to Start? 9

2: It's All About Ability – Or Is It? 31

3: The Happiness Factor and Change 53

4: Understanding Living 'At Cause' or 'At Effect' 85

5: Crushed But Not Broken 101

6: Self-Doubt – Fear of the Unknown 133

7: Learning and Growing 149

8: Understanding People, Understanding Self 165

9: What is the Real Value of Goals? 185

10: Success 207

11: Is It Okay To Accept Your Circumstances? 223

12: Everything Happens For A Reason 235

Conclusion: The Full Circle 245

RESOURCES	261
The 4 Levels of Happiness	262
Steps to Writing an Affirmation	263
Steps to Success	264
A Quick Guide to Goal Setting	265
Your Lifestyle Circle	266
About the Author	271

Preface

When I think about how I came to write *The Full Circle*, it strikes me as it is quite funny. I had never intended to write a book in my life and yet, here it is. Several years ago, I was speaking with a friend of mine and we were discussing our life goals. During the conversation, she told me she had thought for many years that she wanted to write a book. It was burning inside of her, but at that stage, she had no plans to make it happen. I felt it was an amazing dream for her.

I can almost hear the exact words I said in response when she shared her goal with me. "That's fabulous" I said, "but it is the last thing I would ever think of doing. I have no goal of writing a book and wouldn't even consider it, but, I wish you all the best. I feel excited for you and I look forward to reading it when you finish. I can't wait."

So, with all my hesitancy and doubts on the subject, you might ask how this book came about. Well, through my personal development work, I often met with many people and teachers in seminars and retreats. In one seminar I attended, a woman came to speak about her book writing course. A lady I was sitting next to (who subsequently became a friend) was very interested in the course; however, she couldn't afford it. The instructor, Emily, then told us that she would allow a "two for one" deal if that would make it easier for people to join her in the program. That's all it took. I asked the lady, if I signed up, would she be able to afford participating? I must have been having a moment! She said "yes" and, consequently, we both attended the course together. That was nearly five years ago.

When I attended the classes, I had no idea what I was going to write about, along with a great deal of the other participants. I started to have thoughts about my life. I had been married twice and, after my second divorce, I felt totally disempowered. I thought about what I considered to be all the injustices I had suffered throughout my marriages – how I had been treated, the lies and cheating – and considered writing about that.

After careful thought, I realised it was not about someone else, it was about me. I was extremely depressed and had a very low self-esteem for many years, even before my divorce. I was very low at times, wondered if there could ever be anything more for me and if I could manage on my own? The great thing is that I have been able to live again in a much better place than ever in my life. Once on my own, I started my personal development work. I became responsible for my own life. I became an individual who, in a few years, had transformed my life to be the best I can be for myself and those with whom I interact.

When I started the lessons, these thoughts must have been bubbling just below the surface because I now had a vision. For a long time, I had wanted to help women change their lives to more positive and empowered ones, but I was not sure how to do that apart from my coaching work. I did want to reach out to women who may have been in a similar situation to me – women who had been dealt an ugly blow – perhaps by facing the death of a spouse or divorce, becoming an empty nester or finding themselves alone for any number of reasons. In some other cases, sickness, disability struck, or they were unemployed and wondering if they would ever get another job at their age. And, if they are able to, what would they offer?

Whatever the case, there are many women out there who are in this horrible place not knowing if they can have it any different, and if they can, how would that happen? They have lost their power

Preface

and do not believe they can ever get it back. In many cases, fear of the unknown or of being alone may have crippled these women, preventing them from making a change. It had happened to me - I figured I was not alone in this. I wanted to help others become the wonderful women they were meant to be — living on their own terms and empowered once again. So, I got out of my comfort zone and tackled the job.

Writing *The Full Circle* has been cathartic for me and I have learnt so much more about myself and what makes me 'tick'. This is part of the reason why it has taken almost five years to write the book. Many times, going over my life and reliving certain experiences has been quite painful. I needed time out frequently. Every time I came back to the book, I found I had grown and grasped more. I went deeper into my thoughts and emotions and felt I was giving more each time which I hoped, in the end, would help others.

My mission is, ultimately, to have every woman on this planet empowered to choose and live the life they desire. I will do everything in my power to make this happen for each and every person in my life. I want to help women take what they can from their life lessons — as well as those of others — and learn from them. From this, hopefully, they will see what they thought was the worst that could happen may, in fact, be what helps them grow stronger and more successful than they possibly thought. I have the desire to help as many women as possible to find their feet, claim their power and regain their lives. Just for interest, I have been the first from that book writing class to finish my book! That in itself is amazing!

Introduction: My Circle Begins

*"The work itself has a complete circle of meaning and counterpoint.
And without your involvement as a viewer, there is no story."*
– Amish Kapoor

There is something wonderful about circles – never knowing where they start or end (they really seem to have no beginning or end) – yet they connect and draw in many different thoughts and ideas. A dictionary describes a circle as a round shape whose boundary consists of points at equal distances from the center. Coming "the full circle" is having completed a cycle and returning to the starting point.

A circle is a universal symbol with far-reaching and sometimes profound meanings. In all cultures, circles represent the universe and other celestial objects. The North American Indians were deeply spiritual and communicated much through the circle symbol, with meanings taken anywhere from the seasons, the circle of life and death, rebirth and the four elements – earth, air, fire and water. Other meanings of circle symbols can be closeness, protection, focus, wholeness, infinity, mobility – the list goes on. This is not a book about the meaning of circles. However, when one looks at the extensive meanings and symbolism of the word, it puts a whole new slant on why the title *The Full Circle* came about.

The Full Circle

Before I begin, I would like to say that while sharing some of my story, my intention comes out of the highest respect for all those who have been influential in my life and for those who have ultimately been part of my journey. Without them, there would be no story. When I referenced certain people, it was done with love and for the purpose of sharing real life experience and wisdom with the women reading this book.

From birth until I was nine years old, my family lived in a suburban area in the United States. My father worked a job while my mother was a stay-at-home mum. She would be up early getting chores done, getting my sister and me off to school; and then she would do her volunteer work and socialise until it was time to get ready for the end of the school day. Her day continued to be full with after-school activities, homework for us kids, dinner, bedtime and so on. That was how I saw the average American family functioning. Then my father was posted overseas, and everything changed. With it came upheaval and a complete lifestyle adjustment.

This was definitely where my "circles" started, as I had to learn to make the sort of change that was alien to me. Being torn away from my neighbourhood and school was hard enough. However, I not only left the city and State that I had lived in, but the country as well.

The first move took the family to Switzerland. Within a year we moved again, this time to Australia. With these moves came loneliness, a feeling of not belonging, as well as feeling lost in my life. There were many times I was made fun of because I dressed differently, did not speak the language (French while in Switzerland), or had a different accent (as was the case in Australia). In Australia, especially at the time, the prejudices were quite extreme. Nowadays, the United States does not seem as far away from Australia as it did then, and Australians, on the whole, are more accepting of foreigners. However, when I arrived at the age of ten, it was a different experience.

Introduction: My Circle Begins

Being uprooted over those years, to not just another country but a different continent, was quite traumatic. This although strengthened me in the long run. Nevertheless, because of the moves, travel became a significant part of my life. Until I returned to Australia many years later as an adult, where I took up permanent residence and eventually gained citizenship, the circles of my life continued. Before this, I had gone back to my roots to live in the U.S. to finish high school and attend University. I moved to several different states and travelled extensively throughout Europe. During this period, I no longer lived with my parents, yet I still seemed to be 'on the move' and not settled in my life. As in my past, the circle of loneliness and the feeling of not belonging snuck in until I adjusted to my new surroundings.

I have had what I would consider a normal sort of life and, while interesting in many ways, my story is not full of earth-shattering experiences. So, what is so inspiring about my life? I have had many trials and some very low periods. At one time I was happy, healthy and secure – then all that changed. In the second half of my life I became very, very low. Was my life meaningless, as I felt so often that it was?

Perhaps you have felt that way at times, too? Do any of us really have a story to tell? If you are not rich and famous, or have not been faced with extreme adversity, you may feel normal too. I would like to say that this book is written for all those women who may be like me. We are not rock stars or Nobel Prize winners. We have not been caught in a tsunami or lost a limb. But we certainly have hit rock bottom and we want to return to our old selves and thrive once again. We want to find our feet, claim our power and regain our lives, but we are stuck. We do not know the way out. We may be 'normal'; however, that is what makes this book so important. We 'normal' women are in the majority. We are struggling through life, having lost our purpose. We feel as if we are insignificant and ordinary, but we are not in the minority here. Those women who have lost a limb, become a rock star or been caught in a tsunami are in the minority. This means that there are so many more 'ordinary' women who have lost their way and need help getting their lives in control again.

As I write this, I do not know exactly what your journey through life has been. You may be facing major health issues or divorce. Perhaps you have lost your partner and you are now alone. You may have come through – or are still living with – domestic violence or some form of abuse. You may have become an empty nester or lost your job. You may be feeling as if your family and/or your life are falling apart. Whatever it is for you, I want you to know that I am here for you, to help you make that full circle journey and find your purpose once again.

> *"It is the journey and experience of learning that is most worthwhile in ultimately finding your purpose and happiness once again."*
> **– Paulette Archer**

I am occasionally astonished that people think I have led such an interesting life. To me, my life has been just a normal, ordinary one. However, as I started travelling early in my life, it was undeniably interesting. I have certainly met some wonderful men and women, had many astounding experiences, and travelled to many fascinating places over the years. My perception of normal, therefore, will most likely be quite different from yours.

Until I first left the U.S. and started travelling, my life was much the same as that of my friends and relatives. Once the travel began, the same held true. Yes, I was travelling and experiencing a new life in a foreign land. However, while living that life, I was experiencing the same things as my peers. For me, that felt normal and ordinary with nothing special about it. I went to school, did my homework, visited

Introduction: My Circle Begins

with friends, ate and slept. Travel became the norm. While living in Europe, travelling from country to country was something that could be done for lunch – it was quick and not perceived as special for Europeans.

Can my normal life be extraordinarily inspiring if I had not won a gold medal, accomplished a world record or overcome a major disability? This question led me to think that being famous is not what life is all about. I have discovered that there are many people whose normal – and perhaps ordinary – lives have imparted a fabulous message to this world. Inspiring others is about making the most of what you and I have. It is about knowing what is right for me at this time in my life. And if it is not – if change is what I want – then change is what I can have.

If you are at that place in your life where you want change or feel you need change, maybe there are circumstances holding you back – fears, insecurities, unknowns. You may not feel you have the strength to make those changes, or you just do not know where to start and feel you have no support to change your life. If that is the case, I would like to invite you to journey with me and discover for yourself the keys to unlocking change, finding your feet, claiming your power and regaining your life. While doing so, you will find that you will go the full circle more than once – as I have done.

"Between stimulus and response there is a space. In that space is our power to choose our response. In our response lies our growth and our freedom."
– Viktor E. Frankl

By the time you reach your 40's, you will likely have figured out that life does not always pan out as planned. In fact, most of the time it doesn't fit into the perfect mould we dream of.

The Full Circle

Do you accept your life as it is or reject it? How are you dealing with failures or setbacks? Have you become the victim or do you step up and find solutions so you can take control of your life? How you adapt to the changing circumstances in your life can make all the difference in whether you feel fulfilled or frustrated.

For a number of years, I lived at effect – meaning that I did not take responsibility for my own life. After moving back to Australia in my late 20's, I married a man who already had children. I struggled to fit into the role of step-mother – a role in which I never felt worthy or accepted.

Years later, I became distressed at my own difficulty in conceiving my first, and then my second child – having a seven-year gap and fertility treatment for both. My work life was miserable since I had left my nursing profession to be available when needed in our family business. Although I wanted to be successful working in the business, I did not work full time and had difficulty identifying with it. I was expected to help when needed, but, despite the equal shares and the same financial contribution I made, I had very little control or say in the enterprise.

Another huge issue for me was being separated from my entire family once I had moved back to Australia. I had no relatives in Australia and did not get back to the U.S. to visit my family for several years. My marriage suffered, and I experienced many conflicts which stemmed from all these situations. By the time I reached my late 30's, I started to feel powerless and unable to change.

All in all, taking responsibility was not my strong suit and, what was worse is that I had no idea I could. Then something changed everything! My worst fear became evident when, after 27 years together, my husband left me. I was alone and somehow had to find a way to build a new life for myself. As devastating as that experience was at the time, I can look back now and say with confidence that it was one of the best things to happen in my life. I believe that

Introduction: My Circle Begins

everything happens for a reason. I know with certainty that I would not be the strong, confident person I am today if I had not worked through that experience – as hard as it was at the time.

This book relates some of my life story and what I have mastered through these experiences. It no longer is a normal life. It is full of circles of change for me. Through what I have achieved, I trust this will inspire you to take control, find your feet, claim your power and regain your life.

The Full Circle is a journey of learning experiences. I continue to grow as I become more aware daily – and you can, too. I have confidence that you will gain insights from my experiences. Perhaps you will even step out of your comfort zone and, in the process, find the contentment you seek in life. I have encountered many of the challenges that you may be experiencing now, and although I considered myself a strong person overall, I hit rock bottom and could see no way out for a very long time. I did not envisage any light at the end of the tunnel – it was all darkness. I had no love for myself nor placed any value on my life. I did not care if I lived or died.

Even though I still have challenges, I have found my purpose. I now love myself and have found many ways to deal with situations which previously would have brought me down. I am healthier and happier than ever before in my life. I treat my challenges as learning experiences. I can take every situation and make it positive. My journey continues, and now, when I fall down, I can pick myself up, dust myself off and move on. My wish is that you find inspiration from reading this book to find your purpose once again and bounce back into a wonderful life worthy of you.

This book is intended to be interactive because it is just as much about you as it is about me. In sharing parts of my story, you will be able to draw strength and inspiration from it even if your personal experiences have been very different from mine. As you read through the book, you will find highlighted sections which give you an opportunity to evaluate how you feel or think about the topic at hand. Answers to questions and your thoughts can be written into *a journal* as you read and work through *The Full Circle*. There are also spaces within the book where you can jot down your thoughts. By doing this, you will be creating a valuable personal resource that you can refer to later in your life. Your circles will repeat, as mine have, and it will give you an opportunity to reflect on the changes and improvements in your life and also, to see how far you have journeyed over time.

As I share my experiences, I trust you will enjoy the journey with me, and in the process, discover more about yourself so that ultimately, you can choose the life you desire. As I have found, this journey may not always be pleasant. It can be confronting to look back on those experiences in your life that may have been particularly traumatic. Take time out if that is necessary, but **do not** give up. As often as I had wanted to give up, I didn't. I kept on. It has been worth it, as you will find while reading through these pages.

Remember to write down answers to the questions throughout the chapters. Take time to reflect on where you are in your life. I designed the exercises and questions to help **you**. The more deeply you reflect on each one, the deeper your transformation and healing can be. If change is something you want, think of what could be holding you back from making this change. As much as this is *my* story, this will be *your* journey. Keeping your journal is immensely beneficial in your healing process. This, on its own, can inspire you to step up to meet even greater challenges in the future. What do you say? Shall we get started?

"You just stay the course, and do what it is you do, and grow while you are doing it. Eventually it will either come full circle, or at least you will go to bed at night happy."

– Jon Bon Jovi

1: Love, Is There A Better Way to Start?

"Where there is love, there is life."
– Mahatma Ghandi

So where did the full circle of my life begin? With love, I believe. I was conceived because of the love my two parents had for each other, and I was showered with love from them all of my life. Growing up and loving myself was not something I gave much thought to because I always felt loved and secure. At birth I was diagnosed with a heart murmur. While it was not life threatening, it did mean I had to be cautious as a young child. When I started school, I could not participate in most sports and instead, had to sit out and rest. I was never blamed for being unwell as if it was my fault, and I do not believe I ever used illness to curry favour. Often times we hear of people using an illness or disability to elicit sympathy or getting more than anyone else. I did not want anyone to feel sorry for me. As a child, I wanted to be out playing and running around with everyone else. I certainly did not enjoy being forced to rest.

This could have been an excuse to demand attention, but it wasn't. A lot of this had to do with the approach my parents made towards my health. Yes, I had physical limitations and had to be cautious, but I was never blamed or made to feel that I was disabled in some way just because I was not able to be as active as other children. I felt very loved and protected. This is where the need for me to be loved, protected and looked after started.

The Full Circle

My upbringing was by suburban standards normal until my father's job had him posted overseas when I was nine years old. This meant that from time to time, we moved to different foreign countries. Once in the new country, he still travelled a lot for work and was often gone for extended periods of time. While I loved my father, because of his absence, it was my mother who had the most impact on my life at this time. As far as my mother was concerned, she was a determined lady who pulled no punches and called a spade a spade. I think I took after her more than my dad who always seemed more diplomatic!

Because of my dad's work, my mother was the one who really took care of us girls and made most, if not all, of the decisions for the family. My father was the worker while Mum stayed home and instilled most of the values we had and adopted. My dad was a wonderful man, everybody thought the world of him and he definitely had his say – he certainly was not a mouse. It was just that he was absent much of the time. I know my parents talked and discussed their plans. However, in those days, long distance communication was difficult. Decisions often had to be made without discussion and, as a result, my mother was quite autonomous. I developed my earlier independence from her. As far as love was concerned, she had plenty to give and not a day went by without me feeling very loved.

I was the younger of two girls. My sister is two and a half years older than me. From as far back as I can remember, stories were told about how she did not want me when I arrived – after all, she was the Queen Bee and then a baby sister arrived to spoil her life! This was, of course, a very common reaction for a two-year-old. Throughout the years together, we experienced the typical sibling rivalry, yet loved each other very much. We always shared the same bedroom and attended the same school. It was inevitable that we got on each other's nerves at times. Despite this, we did have a strong bond and she would always look out for me.

1: Love, Is There A Better Way to Start?

In the first month following my family's relocation to Switzerland, my sister and I were placed in a boarding school to help us learn French, after which we started our school year at another all French school. Because learning a new language had its own challenges and everything seemed foreign, the fact that we had each other through this experience brought us closer.

Our mother helped us immensely to adapt to each new environment. She would always tell us how she loved to travel and get us all excited about experiencing new places. When we relocated to Australia (after less than a year), my sister and I were initially enrolled in boarding school. This time, because of our classes, we were on separate campuses. I felt somewhat lonely since I was separated from my family, but I did assimilate and made friends easily. As I graduated to high school and was no longer a boarder, my sister and I shared the same campus and spent quite a bit of time together once again.

I have fond memories of those first few years of life overseas, especially while in Australia, despite often being lonely and missing family, friends and those things with which I was familiar from the U.S. This time in Australia was also the last time the family spent much time together. From then on, our family unit changed.

As my sister moved towards graduation, my parents decided to send her back to the U.S. so she could complete high school there. I was 14 at the time. From then onwards we rarely lived on the same continent. Perhaps our relationship has been better as a result. Instead of living on top of one another and driving each other crazy, we could instead remember the excellent times together. It was a way of focusing on all the good in our relationship. We loved and missed each other and made the most out of the times we were together.

Before I finished high school, we moved back to Switzerland. My sister had remained in the U.S. to attend university. Although we are quite different in many ways, we have love and mutual respect for each other. We have not been through many of the same things in our lives, but we are supportive of each other when needed. We are still very close even though we are separated by distance.

> **Consider those closest to you in your life and**
>
> 1. **Take out your journal** and, when answering the questions, leave a space to fill in the answers for each of these people
>   a. Next to each person's name, write down 1-3 things you love about them.
>   b. How you feel when you are with each of these people.
>   c. How you feel about each person when you are not with them, but when their names come up.
> 2. If someone were to interview them and ask about you:
>   a. What do you suppose they would say?
>   b. If they were asked to talk about your best attributes, what do you believe they would be?

My mother seemed quite independent during these early years abroad. Although I felt loved, there were times I felt lost, lonesome and had to get on with my life unaided. Spending time in boarding school was not always easy, but I believe it helped me develop the independent nature I had in my early adult years. I attributed this to watching my mother who pretty much ran the household due to my father's working life. She was a wonderful role model for me.

As you will see later, I became fearful of my inability to be alone and the change that came with it. The thought of being independent then was frightening. Like my sister, my parents wanted me to finish my schooling in the U.S. and attend university there. So, when they

1: Love, Is There A Better Way to Start?

were due to relocate once again – this time to South America – we parted ways. At the time, all I wanted was to move with them and to stay in the family unit. However, they felt my education back in the U.S. was more important.

At this time, that sense of loneliness and having to be in boarding school once again and away from family returned. I saw little of my parents, as well as my sister, from that point onwards. Did I still feel loved? Yes, I did, except that the constant reinforcement was no longer there. Communication back then was quite different from what we enjoy today. Even though there were phone calls and letters, they were far and few between. This marked the end of my life living full time with my family and the circles of change continued.

Entering into university, I had a good level of self-esteem. It was there that I met my first husband. When we met, we had a common bond in that both of our fathers worked for the same company and we were born in the same state. We enjoyed spending time together and could spend hours talking to each other without noticing that time had passed. He became my best friend, my soul mate. He was kind and sensitive and I found him fascinating. He was very supportive of me. When he chose to move to a different state to complete his degree a year later, he asked me to join him. We were married the following year. I was just 20. Was I looking for a replacement for the love, support and closeness I had known with my family the reason I got married so young? Perhaps.

Ironically, it was this longing for family closeness that led to the demise of that marriage a few years later. My husband and I hit a stalemate over the decision to have children. To me a large part of my definition of love and marriage involved family. It was inconceivable to not want to have children. My husband, on the other hand, was determined that children were not part of his plan for the future. In time, I made the heart-wrenching decision to leave him. I thought I could not face a life without the prospect of children even if it meant leaving the person I loved. This circle of love, support and togetherness was the closest to a family that I had and it was now gone.

At this time, my parents were still stationed in South America. I went there, initially, since I felt I had no reason to stay in the U.S. I also needed to have that parental bond and love rekindled. I yearned to be loved and needed. Shortly thereafter, I headed for the place where I had fond memories. I went back to Australia. At this point, I was in my late 20's and, for the most part, alone. Without a doubt, it was a result of my choices. Looking back now, I have no regrets, although I had wondered if I had made the right decision at the time.

While it was not entirely my choice, I essentially left home at age 16 and never again lived with my parents' full time. I often visited them and we enjoyed each other's company, but South America was never home for me. Their intention was that I get a good education and remain in the U.S. While I did finish high school and attend university and get married there, ultimately, I made my own choices about where I would settle.

Now that I am a parent myself, I acknowledge that sometimes decisions are made in what is thought to be your child's best interests and so are made out of love. Still, as the child, it does not always feel like it at the time. My parents were like most I imagine – they wanted to look after me and do what they thought was best for me. For them, that included ensuring I had a good education and stability. Nonetheless, having me living in the U.S. while they were overseas was unstable for me. If I think back to my earlier childhood, I can say confidently that I always felt looked after and loved by my parents, albeit alone.

Can You Start Life Without Love?

Love is a word that is widely used, yet often not really understood as it can have a variety of meanings. When I reflect on my existence, the

1: Love, Is There A Better Way to Start?

starting point has to be love because, as I look back, the occasions where I felt most loved have, without a doubt, been the highlights. Originally when I was thinking about writing *The Full Circle*, I had a picture of starting from the beginning of the time when I struggled in my second marriage and finishing with enlightenment – where I was after learning more about myself. However, as time progressed, I realised my life started at birth with lots of love and over time when there were challenges, love got me through until I hit 'rock bottom' years later. Consequently, I didn't feel loved or loveable.

My journey is one of growth, change and some quite profound personal development. Therefore, the more I thought about it, the more I kept coming back to earlier times when there was always love. At that stage, there was no hate, bitterness or criticism. Instead, I felt content and cherished. It also made me wonder – if that was how my life started- how did it take a nosedive to an extreme feeling of being unloved? And how would I manage to get back to a life of love and happiness once again?

If we can look at situations in my life as a circle repeating itself, I could see that I had a rebirth of sorts. I went back to the beginning of my life, or the beginning of a circle, through my personal development work, which I speak of throughout this book. I looked at what parts instilled feelings of love and security for me. I looked at all of the influencers and could see they were the same people in my circle of life. They were my family and those friends I felt closest to.

The Full Circle

> If images come to mind when you hear the word love
>
> Think about and describe them so a clear picture is seen in your mind's eye.

_____

_____

_____

_____

As I contemplated more, I realised it really was not that simple as there have been more than one circle in my life. I have not embarked on this journey of growth just once – each experience I had, taught me something new. Periodically, I revisit the same lessons through similar experiences, and there are many times it feels as if my life experiences have gone full circle.

Sometimes, just when I feel I am at the end of a learning experience, another emerges – as if another layer of the onion is peeled back. So, with each full circle experience I am gaining new meaning as I grow and develop. With love in the beginning, which was completely unconditional from my parents; the circle of my life went round, alternated by the feelings of neglect - where I felt unloved. This happened in the second half of my life because I did not love myself. Hence, I felt unworthy of receiving any from anyone else. After time spent on my personal development, I learnt to love myself – which completed the love circle as I loved myself and felt the love around me.

Getting Back to Love

Just as life is not as simple as we would hope, I have found that neither is love. At different stages, it will have an array of meanings for you as it did for me. There are many aspects to love: people, experiences, tastes, sights, sensations. Ultimately, love is about you; what you cherish and what is important to you. The most important association of love, however, is self-love. Self-love, is taking care of oneself, looking after one's health by eating well, getting plenty of exercise and resting when needed. It is also about acknowledging one's success and learning from one's experiences, whether good or bad. It is about enjoying life and all it has to offer. It is self-acceptance. Self-love is accepting oneself – warts and all. It encompasses one's physical being as well as one's emotional state.

"Without self-love it may be very difficult to give or receive love from others."
– Paulette Archer

Technically, love can refer to feelings, states or attitudes you or I may have. It can be a strong emotion or something that you are attracted or deeply attached to. Personally, love can bring up a multitude of associations. The term 'love' can reflect how strong my emotions are for certain people or objects. It can imply that I desire a person or object for myself – meaning I want to be with that individual: devour or have strong feelings for the object of my love.

To highlight what I mean, here are some phrases that serve as examples:

"I love my beautiful children and am so proud of them."

"I love my sister dearly; she means so much to me."

"I love to eat gelato and would eat it every day if I could."

"I love to ski and be in the beautiful mountains."

"I love the smell of popcorn at the movies; it reminds me of my grandparents."

The Full Circle

"I love to listen to beautiful music, it's relaxing and enjoyable."

"I love how being outdoors makes me feel – exhilarated and free."

What these phrases illustrate is that we can love much in so many ways. Yet, I have to question: Do we truly understand love and the value that it holds for our lives?

> **YOUR feelings about love**
>
> Set aside some personal time to consider this so you can genuinely feel deeply about your answers. **Use your journal** to record your answers in order to revisit them at a later stage. Give careful thought to each of the questions. When working through them, make sure you can do so without interruption.
>
> 1. When you look back on your life, are there times that stand out where you remember feeling really loved? What were they?
> 2. If you felt loved in the past and no longer feel that way, what has changed for you?
> 3. What do you think you could implement to get back that feeling of being loved?
> 4. What does self-love mean to you?
> 5. How do you feel about your current occupation or position in life? Is it different from what you imagined you would be doing? Does this affect how you feel about yourself?
> 6. Do you love yourself more or less because of your current status in life?
> 7. Do you love who you are right now?
> 8. If not, what would it take to make you worth loving?

Of course, men and women can be fickle when it comes to love, meaning often times they go from one thing to another too quickly and easily. If they do not get immediate gratification, they just toss this new thing out. What they 'loved' immensely an hour ago is now sadly cast off like a dirty shirt. This may not seem like a big deal when you love chocolate ice cream one week and vanilla the next, but when this approach to love becomes a habit, it can impact the way humans relate to one another.

There are a multitude of reasons why people are fickle. Love is complex simply because there are so many levels to it, especially when it comes to love for one another. If you do not know what you are looking for in life and are confused about your values (which I will talk about in depth later in the book), you may fall in love with someone and then, a short while later, you meet someone else who you think would be better for you so you break up with the first person. Your uncertainty about your life leads to your quick change in partners. Low self-esteem, which is your overall emotional evaluation of yourself, can compel you to change your mind about your love relationship. We talk about self-esteem in depth later.

There may be unrealistic expectations when you enter into a relationship. This could be avoided if you take the time beforehand to understand more about yourself and the person you fall in love with. As stated by Dr. John Gray in his book, *Men are from Mars, Women are from Venus*, relationship problems occur between men and women because there are fundamental psychological differences between the genders. Unless you understand what makes you act and react the way you do, as well as how the opposite sex does, misunderstandings and conflict become inevitable. This impacts how you handle your love relationships.

Fundamentally, it starts with the ability to love yourself. When you start to appreciate and love yourself, you recognise your value.

Once you succeed with that, your eyes are unveiled to appreciate other people's values – not in a monetary or social connection sense, but simply being able to appreciate who they are as people. If you expand your perspective and start to take in more of the world around you, you will understand that every experience or encounter can teach you something. Everyone – including those you do not necessarily get along with – may positively add to you. When you learn to love yourself, you naturally start to develop a love for humankind. Ultimately, even people considered enemies can be loved and positively influence you.

Your feelings on self-love

(Even though this book is about sharing some of my story, the main purpose is for my story to help *you* change those things you would like to change about yourself.)

Work through each of the following questions and **write down the answers in your journal**.

1. How important is love to you? Rate it on a scale of 1-10 (1 being the lowest and 10 the highest).
2. How important do you think it is to love yourself? Rate it on a scale of 1-10.
3. Are there factors stopping you from loving yourself? If yes, list them.
4. How would you feel about yourself if those things were not an issue in your life anymore?
5. Do you think if you loved yourself more your life would be different? Why or why not?
6. Do you feel like you deserve to be loved? Why or why not?

Is 'Loving Me' Really That Important?

Learning to love yourself is what many struggle with. Countless people will not even think of including 'self-love' in their category of love. We are led to believe self-love is 'selfish'. We are warned off self-love by the thinking that if you love yourself too much you will not care about anyone else. Admittedly, there are individuals who are exactly like that, and I am sure at some point you have encountered a self-absorbed personality. I know I have. But keep in mind that someone like this exhibits an extreme type of self-love and you should not let the fear of becoming egotistic/narcissistic stand in the way of discovering and learning to love yourself in a healthy manner.

Healthy self-love means you care for yourself physically and mentally; and take responsibility for your actions and life. You respect yourself and know what your strengths and weaknesses are so you make the right choices. You are not arrogant and egocentric; rather you are realistic and honest. If you do not love yourself, you cannot give completely to others. If 'loving you' is missing on the list of persons or things you love, it will not be long before you contemplate the impossibility to love others or accept that they love you. This on its own is self-defeating as you cannot share in real relationships, and often the result is a life that seems empty or incomplete so you do not experience the joy and fulfillment of friendships or relationships.

Because many of us do not consider the love for self as important, we go about life never grasping why we feel so empty. I know this from experience, since I lost my love for myself for many years during my late 30's to early 50's. It was not until I learnt (when I started my personal development journey) that it was 'okay' to love myself, that I really saw a change and experienced growth in my personal life. Prior to that, I never heard much about loving yourself, I just know that I felt happy and well-adjusted when the circle of love was around me.

The Full Circle

> *"You must love yourself before you love another.*
> *By accepting yourself and fully being what you are,*
> *your simple presence can make others happy.*
> *You, yourself, as much as anybody in the entire universe,*
> *deserve your love and affection."*
> **– Buddha**

One Way Love

I was once asked if I think there is a love balance in relationships and whether that can affect how you learn to love yourself. My answer is: If we are now referring to love as primarily between people, there is not always a balance. For instance, a parent's love for their children is often unconditional and, yet, their love for each other may not be. Children may not have the ability to return the depth of love their parents have for them since children need to learn to love – which comes from how they are being loved.

An abusive partner/spouse/parent can receive more love than he or she is able to give, even if they spout the words of love and duly apologise after an altercation. Otherwise they would not treat their 'loved one' in such a hateful way. The love in this type of relationship would certainly not compensate for the other. Each love relationship has different individuals who all have differing capabilities for love, and many would not be in balance.

On a more personal level, how would I know if my husband or partner loves me as much as I love him? How could love be measured anyway? Could it be by giving, caring, sharing and supporting? Or are there other measures? Remember individuals express love in different ways.

Balance comes in understanding the other person and how they love. It is quite possible for one person to love another in a much different way. In my own case, the love my parents, sister and children have for me is totally unconditional and proof of it is not needed. I know that the love other people in my life have for me is also unconditional. This is evident because those individuals accept me for who I am and do not try to change me – one strong sign for me that there is true love in that relationship.

In my past relationships with romantic partners, the love was different from the above. When I think back, I do not believe my romantic partners' love was ever unconditional. I have learnt that unconditional love is necessary for true love to exist. In my marriages in particular, there were often conditions placed on the love. Love may have been taken for granted in some cases with the thought that "if I am in the marriage, I must love you, so I don't need to say or show it in any other way".

By the same token, saying the words "I love you" did not necessarily make it true. The words may have been spoken because it was expected. Was the giving of gifts a sign of true love or did that occur due to other expectations? Was it done out of the blue or because of a birthday, anniversary or were there other times when these words are said or gifts are given?

There were times that one or both of us in the marriage might have expected the other to dress or act in a certain way in an attempt to change the other person. The conditions may not have always been stated verbally – it was often more a feeling that was portrayed. Now when I think back, there were many situations that the love I thought I gave or received was not true. Mutual respect and kindness for each other is a sign of love that was often missing.

It is sad but true how relationships with others can impact how we feel about ourselves. I know that coming out of my first marriage, my confidence had taken a bit of a knock. Certainly, I had married young, but I had loved my husband. Yet, it still had not worked because we did not have the same goals in life. In my second marriage, I was determined to make it work since it was a second marriage for both of us. Yet, the dynamics of our relationship just did not work. On both sides, promises were broken and, at the end of the relationship, I was broken. I was a shadow of my former confident, independent self. I felt unworthy, un-loveable and I certainly did not have any self-love.

I have talked about healthy self-love already and how I lacked it for a long time. I was not taking responsibility for my actions when I blamed my husband for something going wrong in our lives. If a bad investment was made that I did have some input in, I would want to put the blame on someone else. If the children were being difficult, I felt it was because he didn't do enough. I did not look at my actions. I was all about pointing fingers.

If I suffered from headaches, I was always looking for the reasons rather than accepting I was stressed, and doing something about it. Even if I had believed the stress had to do with the problems as I saw them in our marriage, I could not have been able to change anything and so I lived with it. Not loving myself meant I did not look after my mental health.

Are We Just Too Selfish?

Selfish love is more common in the form of inflated egos. People with inflated egos tend to be arrogant and over-confident. They can also be inflexible and unwilling to consider the ideas and opinions of others as being worthwhile or useful. There are many people who become so self-absorbed that everything is about them and what they want. This type of individual is often very driven and has little or no regard for others. They do not care who they use or trample in order to reach their goals. This is because, for them, love does not include others. It is only about themselves and what they want.

Being in a relationship with an egotistic person, be it a colleague at work, a friend or romantic partner, can be soul-destroying. For the non-egotistic person in the relationship, much effort may be geared towards keeping the other person happy. They give so much of themselves and their love. They may bend over backwards to be accommodating. But instead of getting love or appreciation in return, they just get knocked down by the egotist's thoughtless actions and carefree attitude.

This not only impacts the relationship, it also affects how the accommodating person starts feeling about themselves. They may start feeling they are not worthy of love, and so they stop loving themselves. This certainly would not occur if the person involved truly loved his or herself in the first place. There would be no effort made to keep the egotist happy. With a healthy self-love, you are accountable for your own thoughts and actions – as we saw previously.

Low self-esteem leads to lack of self-love. A past client of mine had a partner like this who made her life quite unpleasant. She had very low self-esteem and due to how she was treated, she had feelings of inadequacy under his constant jibes. Because there was no self-love happening for this woman, we needed to work to gain that back for her so that she had the strength and belief in herself to function effectively as a wife and mother to her children. Happily, in time the situation changed and although her husband is still very self-centered, their relationship is wonderful and he has learnt to love and value her for all that she is – she loves herself more importantly, and him, 'warts and all'!

On the whole there is too little love for others in this world. If I look at the world around me, the population appears to be more self-centered nowadays compared to how I remember when I was growing up. In some ways, this could be linked to our busy modern lifestyles. As much as we love technology, it can cause isolation. Through mobile phones and computers, we can be 'with' someone without really being with them since we are communicating via social media. I have to wonder if this is having an impact on how we see relationships or love.

The Full Circle

Internet communication has many positives – connecting with old friends and allowing individuals to keep in touch on different continents (this is wonderful, since now I can be in touch with my family and friends overseas daily if I desire). Nonetheless, it makes it possible for people to watch their friends' lives without really getting involved. You can follow what is happening on social media platforms such as Facebook or Twitter, so it almost negates the need to pick up the phone and have a real conversation from time to time. There is a lot of one-way communication happening. Is this affecting how we respond to people in relationships? Is our world getting smaller? Do we now love ourselves too much to think of anyone else?

Where Is the Love?

How does anyone become more aware of the love that surrounds you? The answer to this question is that as we become conscious of the love we have for ourselves, we can see something in others. The inward sense of love works itself out as an outward expression of love, and we can then accept what others give us as a pure gift. If we think we do not deserve love, or cannot love who we are, we might view others in the same light. We may even think something along the lines of: "if they don't love themselves then they can't be doing something out of love for me, they must want something". Loving others and accepting love from others really starts with loving yourself. If you think that others are out to get you, you will not be able to receive what they are willing to share.

Ultimately, it comes down to love roots. How you feel about yourself influences how you interact with the rest of the world. If you are insecure, bitter or angry, you are likely to push people away rather than invite love or relationships. At an early stage of my life I felt loved and secure, but sometime later, after two broken marriages, I was quite a different person. I had lost my confidence; my self-esteem was at an all-time low – I most certainly did not feel loved. The questions were: "was there a way back to finding that place of love and security and could my circle of love return"? If the circle of my journey of self-discovery had a beginning, this had to be it.

I had to look inward and outward. I had to discover the love inside of me as well as the love that surrounded me. It was already there. I just had to take the blinkers off in order to see it. As I examined my life, I had to admit that, in the early years of growing up, it had been a good life. While it had been unconventional in that we moved around a lot and travelled, I was always secure in the love that my family gave to me.

My father was the provider and my mother the caregiver. Both of my parents were there for me, no matter the distance. I knew that I could call on them at any time to get the support I may have needed. My sister was there even when we were not in the same school or on the same continent. She understood the life we led, the challenges and the fun times. We would support and love each other even when we were oceans apart.

As I started my journey of self-discovery, I realised that there was, in fact, a lot of love around me starting from a very young age. As far as I am concerned, I think I had the best parents in the world. They made me feel great – beautiful, worthwhile, smart – perhaps everything that means anything to anyone. I could have had one eye in the middle of my head, arms and legs backwards and this would not have been any different. What an awesome way to feel. With any of the health issues I had until I became an adult – heart murmur, frequent tonsillitis, burst appendix – they were always there to get me through. I had a great network of family and friends.

Besides my immediate family, I have many extended family members who continue to keep in touch, no matter the time between visits or distance between us. I still have friends from my earliest life in the U.S., as well as those I had met in my earliest years abroad. Of course, I had an older sister and we grew to love each other and cherish our place in the family as sisters. I believe that this is significant because we really have quite different personalities. Perhaps it is because we simply love each other for what we are and we value each other's lives. Our love is unconditional.

"The ultimate lesson all of us have to learn is unconditional love, which includes not only others but ourselves as well."
– Elisabeth Kubler-Ross

> **Use six words to describe a person worth loving**
> 1. Could those words describe you? Do you want those words to describe you?
> 2. What needs to happen to become the person you would love?
> 3. Create an affirmation about yourself. (See page 263 in Resources for assistance.)
>
> Describe yourself in just six words. The affirmation must be positive and how you feel about yourself and your life, or how you want to feel about it. Once you have written it, read it out loud. How does it make you feel?

_____

_____

_____

_____

_____

At the time I was piecing my life back together, after my second divorce, using the knowledge that I had been so loved helped me to connect the dots. I started to comprehend the importance of love

– not just in the context of relationships, but also in terms of who I was. As I viewed the circles of my life, I could identify the highs and lows. More importantly, I began to identify the importance of love.

If I was to take control of my life – if I was to move forward – I had to learn to love myself once again. If I could love myself, then I would be able to receive and appreciate all the love around me. Happiness and contentment could follow once I was secure in the knowledge that I was worth loving, especially of myself!

My circle of life started with love. So, does love have to do with my abilities in life or is this a new circle for me? Can our self-love be affected by our capabilities or lack of them? Does life itself have anything to do with our ability? These are questions worth asking and contemplating; let's explore them.

2: It's All About Ability – Or Is It?

"It always seems impossible, until it is done."
– Nelson Mandela

When I contemplate this, I am not sure if ability was that important to me as a child. It was not something I focused on. I could either do something or not. If not, I was never made to feel that I was unintelligent. My mother was the one I mostly went to for help. She was always full of praise, supporting and encouraging me, no matter my ability. Her encouragement mantra would be "as long as you are doing your best, you are successful". I felt the love of my parents regardless of any ability I may or may not have had. As mentioned in the previous chapter, their love for me was unconditional.

Sometime after my University days, I became more aware of the importance of developing skills and abilities. I was to learn later in life that not everyone shared this attitude of my parents when it came to measuring ability and/or success. When I had put in my best effort and was treated like I had failed, it hurt. In the second half of my life, I had some teachers and some employers who I felt were less than encouraging. At that time, I looked at bettering myself through reading and expanding my knowledge. At the same time, I did not think I had the ability to do much because I was listening to what others had to say about me.

The circle of self-doubt started. At that stage of my life, I had lost my self-confidence. The incessant thoughts that I was not capable often held me back from trying at all. What I did not appreciate at that stage was that everyone has abilities. It just may be they have not discovered or developed them yet. That one person learns skills faster than someone else does not make the other person brainless or incapable. Just because you do not have a certain ability does not mean you are unable to learn. By the same token, if a person is a genius in one aspect of their life it does not mean they are genius in other aspects. At the time, I placed too much importance on what others thought of me which, by all means, only fueled my low self-confidence.

Think about your abilities

1. What talents do you know you have?
2. What abilities do you think you don't have but would like to have?
3. Make a list which can be altered at any time.

_____

_____

_____

_____

_____

Is Ability Everything – Or Is There More to It?

Ability is important, but what is more important is doing your best. We may have the same chance to learn but we assimilate differently. So, your ability to do a task varies from another person's. It does not necessarily mean you are smart or not, it is just the way you are.

2: It's All About Ability – Or Is It?

Ability is linked to self-confidence. If I am self-confident with a healthy self-esteem, then I have more faith in my ability to do whatever I need to do. I am empowered to do the task with knowledge and enthusiasm and that leaves me with a sense of accomplishment. I feel I am and can be a success. There have been times in my life that I have felt like an ignorant loser and a failure at everything. Had my abilities changed? Or was my self-confidence at that point simply so low I did not believe I could do anything right? The latter is the case.

"Expose yourself to your deepest fear; after that, fear has no power, and the fear of freedom shrinks and vanishes. You are free."
– Jim Morrison

As a child, I did well because I believed in myself. I was child-like – not much consideration to what others thought of me. My parents believed in me as well. I asked my parents for help if I needed it and not once was I made to feel deficient for failing to understand something. When I felt like I did not 'get it', I was encouraged to continue and once again do my best. My parents did not believe in laziness. They encouraged me because they knew I was willing to work at things that I found difficult and really put effort into my projects. I was encouraged to continue and not give up. I learnt the value of perseverance and completing my objectives. Perseverance and determination were worth it. When I did well, I felt wonderful and knew I had worked to the best of my ability. I never gave up.

Entering grade 10, 11 and 12 in high school came with mixed feelings. With the change in schools as I moved to three different countries, the teachers may not have been quite as understanding and did put pressure on me to work hard in order to move into the next grade. In spite of those challenges, I did continue to do

The Full Circle

well in my exams. At least I did not lose time with the moves, even though the school years were not the same, and I graduated at the conventional age.

The circle of ability that was started from kindergarten continued throughout my school days. I went to school, did my homework, had tests, passed and started over again the following year. My competence increased as I got older and studied new subjects. I did not win any awards, but I was a strong and solid student with better than average grades.

One of the highlights which showed that I had some special abilities came when I was at University. I was very proud of the fact that a classmate of mine and I were able to design our own elective subject in an area of nursing of special interest to us. This was done under the guidance of our professor. That the professor was quite willing to support us was a real win. Just to be given the chance to design and complete a semester in this unique course was tremendous. I do not believe this would have been possible without faith in myself and great self-confidence coupled with some ability at least. More so, if the professor had not believed in our (my study partner and I) ability to do such a thing, we would never have been given the opportunity to initiate the elective course.

As I grew older with self-doubt creeping in, I became more inclined to give up when I found something too hard. That age-old conversation which had started in the second half of my life would repeat in my brain: "You can't do it anyway; you may as well give up". So, I would. I would talk myself into the fact that I had bitten off more than I could chew or that I didn't really need to do it anyway. I would then justify my decision by saying: "why bother, I really don't need this" or "what was I trying to prove"? The mind can play strange tricks on us. In giving up I believed I had avoided being a failure – something I feared. In some warped way, this helped to preserve my self-esteem. But somehow deep down there was another part of me that told me I was a failure because I had given up.

What preluded this change in me? It was a combination of factors, rather than a single event. My environment had changed. The people I was closest to had changed. I had changed. Most significantly, I stopped working on developing my abilities because my self-belief took a dive.

Thoughts on your abilities and your life
1. How does your ability to complete a task for instance, impact your life?
2. Have you ever avoided doing something or given up because you surmise you don't have the ability?
3. Have you ever turned out to be proficient in an area that at first you didn't think you could?
4. How did you feel once you mastered the new ability or skill?
5. How did that change how you looked at your abilities and what you want from life?

_____
_____
_____
_____
_____
_____
_____

Trying to Be Perfect

Part of my makeup, at least in the second half of my life, was the need to be perfect – even though I knew this translates into chasing a rainbow. As a child growing up, I do not recall striving for perfection. I felt successful because I had been encouraged and congratulated by my parents when I did well or achieved what I had set out to do. I have been told after my divorce that this was what some people saw in me – my need for perfection. Yet, I know that I have many failings and realistically, I'm far from perfect.

I went through a stage in my life while I was married when I needed perfection. If it was a centimeter short of perfect, it was just not enough. This was, in fact, a symptom of my unhappiness and my need for love and proof of my self-worth. I wanted my children to be perfect as well. I rarely took time out from whatever work I was doing because I did not want to be labeled 'lazy' for taking a break and enjoying myself. I was the first up and last to bed – always making sure everything was done just right in and around the house. Being perfect meant success, which is what I desired. It came back to my ability to do anything and everything. I needed this to be appreciated and loved. I believed this was one way I could show my love and get love in return.

Years later, when my personal development work started, I could see that it is okay to do well and be successful. To be perfect is more of an inhibitor than a motivator for success. I have become aware of how much this idea of perfectionism can and had influenced my relationships with others. If I had a need to be perfect I thought everyone else should be perfect as well – which is just a projection on others because it is really what I desired for myself.

Projection can be described as thinking people can feel, think and be as good as you. If they did not, I felt disappointed. The nagging feeling of disappointment in myself could be attributed to notions that I was not doing my best or that I was being treated as if I was

2: It's All About Ability – Or Is It?

not smart enough to do a certain job. I struggled with that for a long time. But now, although I do strive to be the best I can be for myself and others, I have happiness in my life. I take time off to have fun and enjoy life. I only need to care about what I think of myself and not what anyone else thinks of me. People will always have opinions anyway. So why base my happiness on what they think or approve of me?

It is not possible to reach perfection and I no longer desire it. I am looking at new things that could be of interest to me and if I fail at it, at least I have enjoyed the ride. I am not as upset about those things that do not work out for me as I had been in the past. I no longer say yes to everything asked of me. I make decisions around what I want to do without feeling the need to justify my actions. It has not been easy to change the way I felt about being perfect, but it clearly has been worth letting go of the need to prove myself in the face of success. The circle of the need to please others continued during my marriage and now that circle is to please me!

"Doing your best is what you need to do. Then you know that you are successful.
It is about how you feel about yourself and not what anyone else thinks about you."

– Paulette Archer

> **Consider your thoughts on being perfect**
> 1. Do you sometimes feel the need to be perfect? If so,
> 2. How does this impact your life and the lives of others around you?
> 3. Could it be possible for you to let that go so your life becomes less stressful and happier?

_____
_____
_____
_____
_____

Ability and Failure

Is failure absolute? Does it define who you are? At one point in my life I felt as though it did. I felt as if I had no ability to do anything right. It was a period in my life I felt I was losing myself. These little things added up. I would feel like a failure because I had failed at relationships. There were times, as a parent, when I honestly had not handled a situation in the best way. At other times, I chided myself as being a failure simply because I had given up on something. Besides, I was listening to others' negativity towards me.

These times were low points in my life and not a happy place to be. I felt alone and could feel myself spiraling downwards. The circle of failure started at this time. When these feelings occurred during my marriage breakdown, I tried to avoid doing anything new or asking questions. After the separation, I started taking on a myriad of activities, most of which were geared towards improving my sense of self. At that point, I felt very much like a failure and I just did not want to feel that way anymore! I desperately wanted to find out what made me tick, why I was feeling that way and what I could do to change. Were these things true or was it my inner voice, my lack of self-esteem telling me those things?

Before I left home to finish high school, I always had a desire to make my parents proud. That meant doing my best. Even if I did not quite succeed, my mother's response would be: "you did your best, I'm so proud of you". At that stage of my life, failure was not seen as a negative but a stepping stone in the process of learning. Once I was at boarding school in grade 12 and no longer living full time with my parents, I got into a certain amount of mischief; simple things like smoking, raiding the pantry, meeting up with boys and rebelling against the teachers. There was no need for me to do those things except that I wanted to let down my hair and have some fun – what the restrictions of boarding school did not always allow.

Then on to University where there were virtually no restrictions and I had no one but myself to answer to. I realised I could be responsible, have fun, and still do well at my coursework. I was successful and living on my own showed me that I had the ability to do what needed to be done and have success without my parents overseeing my life.

Of course, we kept in contact through letters (no email back then) but not often. In more recent years, as I have been on my path of self-discovery, I started to appreciate that I had certain abilities. If there was something I did not know, I could learn to do it. If there was a failure, I could learn from it. One of my subjects at University was Chemistry. I worried about it because I thought I would be a certain failure. I therefore worked very hard and not only did I avoid failure, I also finished with the top grade. I had not been told by anyone that I would not do well, I merely did what was needed to be done as well as I could.

In later years, this did not invariably happen. While working in the family business, there were times when it was not smooth sailing.

The Full Circle

Perhaps a customer was unhappy. I would feel like a failure because I took it that it was my fault the problem existed. Once I became an employee later on, the same may have been true. Whose fault was it that something did not go right? It must be mine! Once again, I had failed.

If I was unable to handle a task that perhaps I had experience in, my boss may have belittled me for not knowing how it was done. I was told that I had been given the information more than once and I should know what to do. I was asked: "what good was your degree if you don't even know how to do seemingly easy tasks"? These comments fueled my feelings of being a failure and made me doubt my abilities. When these sorts of occurrences happened, I found myself sinking into the mindset of a loser. I would look for an escape and start to hate my job, not wanting to work there any longer. When that happened, my self-confidence would be gone in a heartbeat.

All of these occurrences in my life that left me feeling like a failure, I realised later, actually had their purpose. Each experience held some nugget of wisdom that I could learn from. It was up to me to take the opportunity to learn from them. I discovered that failure was not absolute and it need not define who I was or what I felt about myself. Failure was only one side of the coin. The other was a chance to learn. The only true failure was not taking something away from the experience, not advancing or learning from mistakes. Even the negative experiences in my life had a part to play. They all had, in some way, shaped who I was. You could even say they were necessary for my development.

Unfortunately, the circle of feeling a failure and lack of ability went round and round for a number of years until I started my personal development work in my mid 50's. It was only when I opened myself up to the possibilities that I was a worthwhile human and developed some self-love, that I really started to learn. I needed to be receptive to the idea that it was all part of who I was and it was all – in the end – good. In the process, I learnt to take responsibility for my thoughts and actions, not just believe what I heard from others. I learnt to trust in myself and my abilities, whatever they were, and to overcome challenges. A saying that has helped me, and that I now live by, is that there is no such thing as failure, only feedback.

Failure or Feedback

1. How do you feel about the word 'failure'?
2. Do you think failure is caused by a lack of ability or a lack of self-belief?
3. When you consider your perceived failures was this because of your ability or your self-belief?
4. If you believed differently could this impact your capabilities? If so, how?
5. Are there times in your life when failure helped you to develop your abilities? How did you grow? What did you learn?

_____
_____
_____
_____
_____
_____

Ability and Action

Nothing in life will be accomplished without taking proper action. Your abilities come from exerting some effort to cultivate your skills. You cannot have one without the other. Lessons to be learnt are just that – you cannot develop, learn and grow, or increase your abilities, without first taking some forward motion. That activity could be studying a course, taking on a new job, learning new skills, practicing for a triathlon, or practicing your piano lessons. Whatever these actions are, they lead to new skill sets and new abilities.

Achieving goals (which we spend more time on in Chapter 9) and going for what you have dreamed of requires some form of action. Are you looking to lose weight and become healthier? Having a goal of starting a new career or acquiring a better income in the job you have? Having better relationships? Or leaving a bad one? These things will not happen unless you set some goals to achieve your weight loss or learn new skills, work harder and apply for that promotion, learn how to better communicate with others or leave the relationship. All of these require exertion.

It is more than likely, if your weight and health concerns need changing, that you have come by these issues over a period of time and taken steps probably in the wrong direction or engaged certain ineffective measures. Adopting the precise steps to change is important. You would have had certain abilities to be in the particular job you are in. Taking action into gaining new skills puts you into a better position for that promotion if that is what you seek. If you are now in a situation where a new job is what you are looking for because you may need a change or have lost your job, then taking up some form of further education can place you in a better position of finding what you are looking for.

Perhaps you are looking to do volunteer work. You will achieve nothing without taking the initiative to search for what interests you. No new relationships will be made sitting in front of your TV every day. You need to get out and meet people, become involved. Perhaps going for counseling will help in your relationships but, if not, taking action to move away from the relationship is advised.

2: It's All About Ability – Or Is It?

Throughout my life, I have taken up quite a number of volunteer positions. In each case, there was a certain amount of learning that went with the work. I enjoyed and found very gratifying most of what I did. There is so much need for volunteers and, if the work you seek is helping others who may be in a worse situation than you, it can be very humbling and gratifying. It put my problems into perspective, which made them less of an issue. After my separation, if I felt I had a hard marriage and was not coping, my work with Crisis Counseling told me otherwise. Commencing work to become a volunteer crisis counselor taught me much about life and other people, and also changed my personal view of it.

Irrespective of the opportunity, action is a fundamental requirement for any ability to transform into reality. By following through with this, results are achieved and your competence can change your way of thinking and your existence. We all have our own special gifts. What one person can do compared to another does not matter. It does not make one person better than another or smarter than another. It just might be that one individual knows more or has a higher interest in a certain subject or area than another. You should not judge or be judged differently because you do not have a certain degree or type of training or job. There are jobs out there for all of us and each of our individual skills.

We are fortunate that not everyone wants to do the same thing. The world would not be nearly as interesting if we all did everything alike. Many situations would be left unattended because we would have no one to do them. We need to be proud of everything we do and more importantly, do it to the best of our ability. I am appreciative of many things in my life and my abilities around them. Am I an expert in those things and better than anyone else? No, not necessarily. But for me they are my achievements which means I can own them and be proud of them.

I discovered I had plenty of capabilities, especially after graduating from University. I am proud of achieving my degree in nursing and being part of that profession. When I took on a position relatively late in my nursing career, it was in the area of IVF. This is a highly specialised area to be involved in. I never thought at my age (then in my mid 50's) I would ever be given a chance to take it up, let alone learn the specialty and be great at it.

When references are made to jobs, housewives and mothers are often left out. No value is accorded those 'professions', yet they are very important and necessary stations in life. For me, being a wonderful mother to my two girls is another area in my life in which I am very gratified. Seeing my girls, now young adults, I know that I have done a pretty good job. Of course, learning to swim and scuba dive at the age of 54 was also a great achievement of which I am very pleased. More recently, taking on a new career and starting my own business has been daunting, although rewarding. If I can help just one other woman see the good in her abilities which can lead her to make better decisions and find her feet, claim her power and regain her life, I will be gratified.

If you have taken action in the past year to develop your abilities/skills, list what you have done

_____

_____

_____

What Is the Value in Taking Responsibility?

Taking responsibility is about deciding what you will do in your life that can positively impact how you live. You are in charge and no

2: It's All About Ability – Or Is It?

one can live your life for you. We will talk more in Chapter 4 about this idea of taking responsibility, which essentially means that you are accountable for whatever happens in your life be it - good or bad. I make choices and I accept the consequences that come with those choices. Taking responsibility is also about what lessons I can learn from my actions. Looking back, I get that there were many situations where I took responsibility and many others where I did not. One of my values (which we will talk about in Chapter 8) is responsibility and job satisfaction. For me, there is much value in taking responsibility.

One of my early jobs in nursing was working in a very specialised area – liver transplants. Patients were there because they were deathly ill and sought their best chance at survival. Survival rates for liver transplants were low since this was quite new at the time in the early 70's (1967 was the first successful liver transplant at my University hospital). Consequently, I took on a huge initiative of offering my best in the hopes that all of my patients would survive and live happily into the future.

I worked hard and long hours, but success was not always guaranteed. I only took responsibility for the work I did. When we lost a patient, it was difficult. One unforgettable experience I had in my work in the unit was when the spouse of one of my patients paid me a huge compliment with regard to working with his wife. Even though the outcome was not good, he still took the time to let me know how much he valued how I worked with her. Taking responsibility for my work ethic was evident here.

When I moved back to Australia as an adult, I could not start working straight away. I first had to wait a year for my permanent residency to come through. When it did, there were no jobs available at the hospitals for my profession as a nurse. I made the decision then that I didn't want to wait for something to come up. I wanted to work and I was willing to do just about anything.

The Full Circle

I came across an advert in the paper for a Customer Service Manager at a Car dealership that specifically dealt with Ford products. I went for the job and, even though I had no experience, I talked my way into getting the job. Knowing I had so much to learn, I put everything into becoming the best customer service manager around. I got well informed and gained much knowledge while I was there. I developed the position together with the other management team and the experience was awesome.

By learning another skill, my abilities changed. Even though I had wanted to work in nursing, I took the initiative to find work and take up an active role in my financial situation. I took this position and made it my own. I was working for someone else but did my very best to achieve superior results for the dealership. I took on the responsibility of creating success for the company which in turn, led to my success. I was also told by customers as well as the staff how my role within the company had genuinely made a difference in the way our customers viewed us. These compliments were truly meaningful.

If I commit to doing a task, it is my duty to do it with a great deal of care and enthusiasm. One hundred percent is given to the task at hand. Anything that is worth doing at all, is worth doing well. This was evident throughout the circles in my life around work. If I have a strong work ethic, then I will be successful in my own eyes. I will also be looked upon with favour by my superiors and be known as a person of integrity. These are the rewards for taking responsibility for myself and what I do in my life, personally or professionally. The values of integrity and responsibility were met at this stage.

In my last job in the area of IVF nursing, I totally immersed myself into learning everything I could. I was proud of the clinic in which I worked. I spoke about it often out of work and encouraged people I knew who could benefit from our services to come for a consultation. I was not getting any monetary compensation for doing those things, yet I did it because I took ownership of that position. I worked hard at being all that I could be to our patients. I was praised, once again, for having a strong work ethic and this made me feel proud of myself that I may have made the whole experience a better one for the client.

Taking responsibility did not always happen, however. During my second marriage, there were many instances where I looked to blame someone else when an outcome was not as I had anticipated. Perhaps a customer was not happy with the service they received, it became the fault of the staff member who provided the service rather than mine as the manager. My husband took on most decision-making around budgeting. When I was questioned about spending, I felt it was his fault because he didn't make a budget or let me in on the planning. I did not take responsibility to ensure a budget was initiated and adhered to so that my business and family were financially sound. When I was in this state, I was not living my values. Little wonder I was unhappy.

It is a good feeling to know you have done a job well. It is hugely encouraging to hear positive feedback from clients. More importantly, it is immensely rewarding to know that you have taken responsibility for everything in your life and are not leaving that up to someone else. Reflecting on this, I see that I learnt from the positive as well as the negative experiences.

At this time, I avow that just because an outcome varies from my expectation this does not mean I am useless or that I cannot learn something from the experience. I might have lost an outcome, but my ability to be successful is still very much intact. What I used to see as a failure or lack of a positive win is just an avenue for me to learn something and move on. When I know that I have done my best, there is no need to beat myself up. When I have not done my best, I strive to do better next time. There can always be a positive angle, sometimes we just need to persevere to find it.

The Full Circle

It is also important to be cognizant of the fact that in any given relationship, there are at least two people involved, which means there are not less than two sets of opinions/experiences to a situation. By being accountable for myself and not the other person - their thoughts, feelings or actions - I can let go of anything other than the part I have to play.

If your self-belief is tied to your abilities

1. How can you change this?
2. Can you change your skills so that it will impact your level of confidence?
3. Could there be one particular area of your life where learning something new might significantly impact your happiness and self-confidence? Why?
4. If the opportunity came to learn that skill, what changes would it bring about in your life?

_____

_____

_____

_____

_____

_____

_____

_____

Diving into the Deep End

If there is one example in my life that links ability with belief and success, it is the story about how I learnt to swim and later scuba dive. Due to my heart murmur as a child, I was not allowed to do much sporting activity which includes swimming. This resulted in my fear of the water throughout my life (interestingly enough, my mother had a fear of the water as well and perhaps I took on some of that in my life since she was so much of a role model for me). Knowing that I didn't have the ability to swim, I envisaged that if I got in the water, I would simply drown.

Very close friends of mine who had taken up scuba diving wanted me to join them. However, I was held back by my extreme fear of being in water (let alone under water) and the fact that I did not swim. I was already in my mid 50's and single. Thankfully, by this time I was in a much better personal space. I had grown so much in a personal way that I thought perhaps I **could** do this. Getting out of my comfort zone happened regularly at this stage. Maybe I could overcome my fear of water and learn to swim. If I could get comfortable enough in the water, I might then learn to dive. My musings along with some motivation from my friends encouraged me to try. I had been challenged so much already that I felt maybe, just maybe, I would be able to actually do this.

There was one thing I knew – it was impossible to say no without trying. The memories of encouraging my own children over the years replayed in my mind. How many times had I said to them: "How do you know you would not like something if you haven't even tried it?". Now it was my turn. I wanted to be a good example and role model for my girls, and so walking my talk was important. It was time for me to overcome my fear of water and learn to swim. The ultimate drive for me was to be able to complete my scuba diving certificate, which was even more of a challenge. A swimming test was a requirement for this. If I wanted to dive, I needed to swim. It

The Full Circle

was that simple. Mind you, I wasn't sure if I really wanted to dive, however, swimming had to come first!

I signed up for private swimming lessons. Starting out was tolerable as the pool I was in was shallow. If I ever felt uncomfortable I could simply stand up. The big challenge was to get into the deep pool – one where I didn't have the security of a shallow bottom. There were many times when my swim instructor told me it was time to move to the deep pool, but I was ineffectual in letting go of my fears. The mind games I played with myself were incredible. I was terrified to a point where I was sweating even though I was already wet from being in the pool. I had convinced myself I would not be able to do it and this belief served only to fuel my fear. If I was inept at getting into the deep pool, how would I ever learn to scuba dive?

I can hardly believe how much energy I wasted to fear. This circle of fear presented itself again. Did it have anything to do with my upbringing? To my lack of ability? Yes, I was afraid of being a failure, as I thought I had been so many times before. Eventually, however, I gave in and went into the deep water, on the condition that I would stay in a side lane so that I could grab onto the edge if need be. In the end, I did not need to. I managed to swim unaided.

If I think of how much time I wasted in the shallow pool being petrified, it astounds me. I had held onto the fact that I was unable to swim for so long that my fear had held me back from actually gaining the ability to swim. Even when I had learnt to float, kick and swim strong strokes, I still did not believe I could do it outside the safety of a shallow pool.

The day I swam in the deep pool, my belief started changing. I genuinely knew how to swim. Once I accepted it, I started to swim more confidently. It was an enormous personal victory, but not nearly as big as the day I completed my swim test for the dive certification. We were required to swim 300m with a mask, snorkel and fins and then tread water for ten minutes. It had been a year since I started swim lessons and, while my confidence was up, some doubts still niggled. Mentally preparing myself, I calculated how many laps I needed to do. Then, once I had psyched myself up, I jumped into the water and started to swim.

I recollect swimming for what seemed forever. I heard people shouting from the side of the pool, but I just kept going. I was determined to pass the swim test. Eventually, I lifted my head enough to see what all the commotion was about. What I saw was an ecstatic group of faces grinning from ear to ear. My dive instructor was trying to tell me something, but I was unable to hear over all the shouts and whoops. Eventually, I tuned into what he was saying: "you've done it! You've done more than 300m, you can stop now". It was unbelievable. After living with this fear of water my whole life, I had conquered it. I had learnt to swim! What a wonderful sight to have everyone else celebrating in my success.

Now I could realise my dream, get my dive certification and enjoy the wonders of the ocean. I had stepped way outside my comfort zone, driven by the desire to do something I had never thought possible or even considered. It proved to me that a lack of ability needn't hold me back from achieving any of my dreams. Ability could be attained and goals scored. If I visualised them and worked determinedly towards them, the sky was the limit. No limiting beliefs would be able to hold me back any more. It was time to look at possibilities, not obstacles.

As a child, ability to me, meant anything that I did, how I played, rode a bike, learnt my lessons, etc. I did not feel and was not made to feel incompetent by my parents. I travelled down that path until I developed limiting beliefs later in life based on what I presumed to be true. This might have been because of what someone had said to me, how I was treated by superiors or even my peers who I regarded as smarter than me. They even told me so at times.

Over the years, while in my 40's particularly, my mind had been filled with doubts regarding what I thought I could or could not do. I had

The Full Circle

also made excuses about these things and hence, would not tackle a new project for fear of defeat. I conceded it was better for me to support my family in their endeavours than try something and fail. I was proud of my family's achievements, but that had nothing to do with my own self-esteem. Before learning to swim, I avoided swimming with the excuses: "I'm afraid of the water" or "no thanks, I don't know how to swim". This, of course prevented me from being inadequate. It did not matter what it was in my life. If I acted as if something did not matter to me, I could fool myself that it didn't. Not doing or trying meant that there was no failure for me.

Once I could swim, (and quite well according to my teacher), I was willing to see how I could learn to scuba dive which would become another new skill. Taking scuba lessons was much less challenging done in a pool, than actually being out there in the beautiful ocean under many metres of water. Once again, I achieved this to glorious self-applause. From that point on, I set the bar for myself higher than in my past. I was determined to continue learning new skills and showing myself that, yes, I can do whatever I choose.

I had the desire and was willing to get out of my comfort zone and thrive. It was time to ignore apprehension with regard to my ability and shake off how others had treated me in the past. Comments made around my lack of knowledge or ability no longer mattered.

I can see the full circle happening with my abilities and/or lack thereof. Throughout all those years, I started with abilities and a strong self-esteem, which I had initially lost. Fortunately, I started over again by learning new skills and believing in myself and my abilities. With the new sense of understanding that I could acquire more knowledge and that I had many abilities inside of me waiting to burst out, I found I now had a new level of happiness in my life.

How does happiness come from change? Turn the page to have a look.

3: The Happiness Factor and Change

"Most people are as happy as they make up their minds to be."
– Abraham Lincoln

As far as happiness is concerned, it can revolve in a person's life. I certainly had a circle of happiness in my life as I moved from varying states of wellbeing. Is happiness just a state of mind? Or, the knack to see the positive potential in every situation? Some people argue that happiness is a choice because you never quite know what life is going to throw at you. Others define happiness as an emotion you experience when you are in a state of wellbeing.

This state of wellbeing could be influenced by your capability, environment and the changes in your life, or the people with whom you are involved. The definition of happiness is not simple because it is so subjective. Happiness relates to how you feel as a person. It is natural, therefore, the definition of happiness and factors influencing happiness will differ from person to person. Everything you need in order to be happy can be found within you. That state of happiness comes to the surface when the conditions leading to happiness occur.

Greek philosopher Aristotle (384BC – 322BC) noted that no one would deliberately choose to be unhappy. The levels of happiness stem from his teachings. The Catholic education resource centre states that a look into Aristotle's writings, and those of later Christian writers like Augustine in *The Confessions*, tells us

The Full Circle

that happiness can have four levels. Robert Spritzer, PhD, in his book *Healing the Culture*, affirms that there are four levels of happiness.

Essentially the Four Levels of Happiness are: Basic, Comparative, Linked to Others and Connection. The following diagram illustrates this:

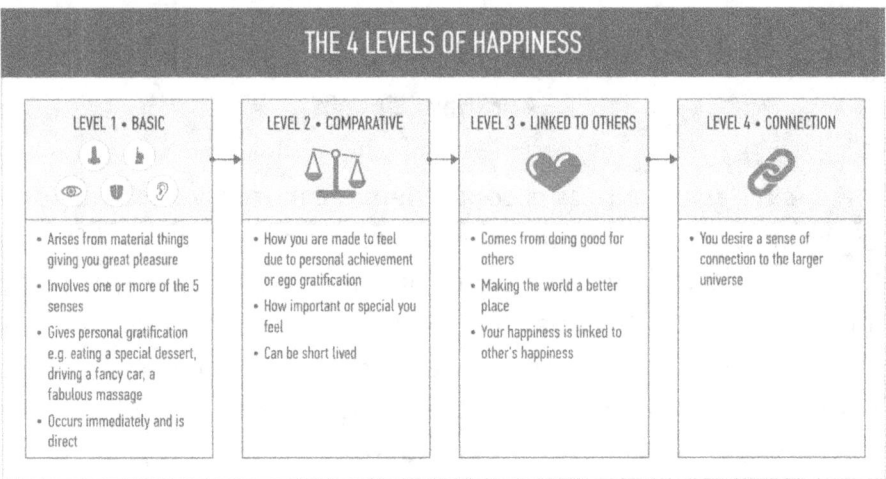

If we were to consider Level 1, many examples come to mind. In this basic level the focus is solely on one's pleasure and happiness from material acquisitions, like expensive perfume or jewelry, or, other sensual gratification. It can indicate a very shallow and meaningless existence. Your happiness in this level can be very strong and short lived. Enjoying these sorts of pleasures is fine unless it is the only source of your happiness.

Level 2 is all about comparisons. It can also be short lived because this level of happiness is dependent on constantly winning and continually comparing yourself to others. An example here could be you winning the finals tennis competition at your local club. Or perhaps you were chosen to represent your company at a conference. Your constant self-promotion can lead to frustration and unhappiness when you don't win.

When we get to Level 3 we start to look away from our own self-gratification and start to consider others. In this level you might be overjoyed because a great friend of yours has obtained their degree at University and can now realise their dream to becoming an engineer. Their happiness is your happiness. This level of happiness is not short-lived as in the first two but can lead to unhappiness when we get hurt by those we may be closest to.

Finally, Level 4 would be considered total happiness if reached. It is the hardest to achieve because we think of it as perfection. However, once achieved we would feel total connection with the universe. If you were to completely immerse yourself in a religion where you might believe you have found the answers to the difficult questions on the meaning of life, you could achieve this connection.

"Happiness is not something ready-made. It comes from your own actions."

– Dalai Lama

Jot Down in Your Journal

What defines happiness for you in your life?

How important is happiness to you?

Defining Happiness

The mental state of happiness begins with positive feelings which range from contentment to immense joy. Let us consider contentment, for instance. This is one state of happiness at the beginning of the happiness spectrum. It is being satisfied with where you are in your life or with what you possess. It can also be a double-edged sword. For some, being content means, you are happy where you are and feel no need to change your situation. You may not feel the need to move out of your comfort zone. I am at a stage in my life where I am content with much of my life, however, I still have a thirst for knowledge and new experiences. I can be content in one area of my life and seek more in other areas. Contentment is the starting platform on my happiness radar.

In my journey I have become content (this differs from a large part of my life, where I rarely felt content and was looking for that which could 'make' me happy). As we will see, happiness comes from within and, until I was happy with and within myself, there would be nothing else to 'make' me happy. I have been able to realise that in raising the bar, stretching myself and understanding more, I can now reach an even higher level of contentment and ultimately more happiness.

My classical example of this was learning to swim. It was a massive step out of my comfort zone. Once I passed my swim test for my dive certification, I was ecstatic! I could not stop smiling because I knew I had achieved something monumental in my life. I had overcome a *huge* fear. I had learnt a new skill and I could now be confident in water. Even getting my dive certification was a magical moment.

That ecstasy I felt when I qualified was however short-lived. With time, it was replaced with a deep sense of satisfaction. For now, I am content with having my open water certification. At a later stage, I may decide I want to advance, which will mean I will have to do more courses. Where I am now with my diving is a good place to be. I am content. This contentment is just one level and type of happiness.

Regardless of how you define it, the emotion of happiness remains one of the most sought-after concepts in life. Mankind will do almost anything in their pursuit of happiness. Sometimes they succeed and other times they find that what they thought

3: The Happiness Factor and Change

defines happiness is just an empty shell. Perhaps in light of this, the question you need to ask is: "What is the value of happiness in *my* life"?

When you consider happiness around the emotion of pleasure, you may be thinking of a wedding, birthday celebration or exceptional moments with the special people in your life. These all give me pleasure. Attending the weddings of my nieces and nephews has been particularly gratifying for me. They gave me opportunities to see my family and friends who I may not have visited for quite some time, and a time to share in their happiness and joy. Significant birthdays are always pleasurable occasions. I can remember my father's 90th birthday. He had invited 90 of his family and friends from near and far for his spectacular party. This was one of the all-time great occasions for all of the guests and my dad shone on the night. What great memories I have from that day!

Pleasurable occasions can be shared as was the case when I surprised my parents for their 60th wedding anniversary. They did not expect me to come to the U.S. from Australia and I know they were totally elated that I had arrived. Being able to bring them such delight and to share their day was wonderful for me. Christmas and other family celebrations, such as christenings, graduations, Mother's Day and Father's Day and anniversaries, as mentioned, are all important to me. Happiness during these times stems from being able to share those moments with significant family and friends in my life

Since I got out of marriage, there have been times when I am alone during festive seasons. Although I thought in the past I would not be happy if this happened, I have found I am quite content. I know that I will not always be able to have my family close to me at certain times, which is no longer an issue for me. In retrospect, it is not just the major events in my life that have resulted in happiness. The small occurrences are worth celebrating - lunch out with friends, attending a special function or going on a picnic in the park.

A big part of happiness has to do with achievement. Some of the times in my life when this was the case were when I learnt to speak French after I moved to Switzerland. I felt a sense of achievement when I graduated from University. When I received my nursing degree, I was ecstatic that I had achieved that goal. Later in life, when I completed my coaching qualifications, I felt that same way.

Being someone who is naturally driven, achievement is certainly a factor in my happiness, and also a part of my values. Values are the core of your being. In other words, your values define you. If your goals are in alignment with your values, they are easier to reach because they become your reason for being, so to speak. It is what you aspire to achieve and become.

There have been times when I have achieved something in total alignment with my values. They may not mean much to someone else, but for me, they are big deposits in my happiness jar. This is because education and learning are highly prioritised on my personal values list. When I am expanding my knowledge base, whether it is for my personal or professional life, I feel a sense of accomplishment and therefore, I am happy within myself. For much of my adult life, I have taken the opportunity to participate in further education, whether out of interest in a particular subject or for something specific to enhance my intellect in my area of expertise. Because I value accomplishment, happiness is sure to follow when they come through.

Over the years, there have been many times I became proficient in something that paved the way to my happiness. I earlier mentioned the time I learnt to speak French. Unfortunately, much of the language has been forgotten. However, when I have an opportunity to give it a go now, I am very happy with my level of understanding. Moving and adapting to new environments, although difficult at times, has found me adjusting quickly and enjoying my new surroundings. My most recent move to a new city was in the past eight years. I have found new ways to meet people and I am participating in activities that I had not tried previously. I quickly became content with my new life.

Many people are satisfied to remain static since change can be challenging, which is quite true. Moving later in life proved that to me. When I was younger and moved, I landed in schools where it was easier to make friends. The times I moved later in life after having children, meant I could meet parents of the children who were friends with mine. This gave me a way to form friendships. Working also affords the possibility of meeting new people and making new friends. Once my children grew up and I was doing less with and for them, a new circle started for me. This circle was by the way the circle of life that I am in now. I meet new people based on the activities and work I do.

Another form of happiness is elation. Elation, to me, is extreme happiness. It relates to those iconic moments in life when you are so happy it seems surreal. For me, two of those elated moments were when each of my daughters were born.

Because happiness is a transient emotion it can be short-lived. The happiness that you gain from a particular moment can appear sometime after the event. Many of you would have a certain level of happiness (perhaps contentment) where you spend most of your time. This will depend on your current situation or expectations.

Your happiness often changes, and you may need to sustain it from time to time. Often, your happiness correlates with your past or present experiences. If something led to your happiness in the past, your expectations would be that the same would happen the next time you experience something similar. Of course, this may not happen. Shortly after my marriage breakdowns, certain occasions did not give me the same level of happiness as they had in the past. Christmas and birthdays were two days I struggled through initially.

> **Consider who controls your happiness**
>
> Take a few moments to sit quietly and work through these questions. **Write down your answers in your journal.**
>
> As you start to unpack the concept of happiness, it is easy to see why it is elusive. Hopefully after considering your answers you will be able to recognise that you are in control of your own happiness.
>
> 1. When do you feel content? Think about those moments. Where are you? What are you doing? Who are you with? Can you put your finger on any particular occurrence that gives you this sense of contentment? Describe it.
>
> 2. Do you spend most of your time living inside or outside of your comfort zone? Have you ever experienced happiness when stepping outside of your comfort zone? Describe the event and why it made you so happy.
>
> 3. Have you experienced moments of pure joy? What were they? Were they shared moments and, if so, with whom?
>
> 4. Does success impact your happiness?
>
> 5. How important is success to you? Write down a moment of success. How did you feel?
>
> 6. How do you feel now recalling that moment?
>
> 7. Have you ever felt so happy and elated that you want to shout and celebrate from the roof tops? What happened to make you feel that way? How long did that sense of elation last?

Happiness is a mental or emotional state in which one feels a sense of wellbeing; it is generally linked to positive experiences. It is subjective and can be linked to both physical and mental conditions. You can experience happiness by being lost in a moment. How many

3: The Happiness Factor and Change

times has a memory of something brought a smile to your face? If I was to think about something one of my daughters said in the past, which brought a smile to my face in the first instance, the same emotional state can happen if I relive that moment in my mind. The physical feelings I may have at this time could be lightness in my body – a tingling feeling all over. I may even have a feeling of goose bumps.

However, for some, these same physical conditions could mean unhappiness. For example, when remembering a loved one who has passed away. The memory may make you smile, but at the same time make you sad, because you miss the person you are thinking about.

As mentioned, your happiness can be linked to your values. This is one of the reasons why happiness is different for each of us. Instant gratification can elicit happiness, but it can also lead to unhappiness if you are receiving the gratification from other means outside of yourself. A classic example of this is drug or alcohol addiction. The transitory high is fleeting and starts a cycle of destruction as people seek to maintain that momentary happiness continually.

In today's modern western society, many people feel they will be happy if they have a big house, a fancy car, a great paying job, tons of money or a fabulous holiday every year. I do not believe this about happiness. I experienced those things and was not happy because of how I felt inside. I realised that for me, to be truly happy it needs to come from within and not from outside materialistic pleasures.

"If you weren't happy yesterday, you won't be happy tomorrow. It's money. It's not happiness."
– Mark Cuban

I have met and coached many people who, when they worked on themselves, found this to be true as well. I believe you can have material possessions and be happy. Though, believing that

The Full Circle

they will automatically translate into happiness will likely lead to disappointment. Material possessions and other things can provide comfort, entertainment and pleasure for a while, but they will not make you happy. Other things that lead to my happiness are acts of benevolence, which means doing volunteer work and being able to give to those less fortunate, which is in the third level of happiness.

Thoughts on your happiness and your values

1. What material possessions 'make' you happy?
2. What do you desire to have that you feel will 'make' you happier?
3. Of all your possessions, which do you value the most and why?
4. If any of them were to be lost or stolen, how would you feel?
5. If you were unable to replace those possessions through an insurance claim, how would you feel?
6. Now that you have worked through these questions on material goods, can you identify what is the true value they have on your happiness?
7. Were you surprised by what you discovered about yourself in terms of the value you place on your happiness?
8. Would you like to change how you regard this fact and if so in what way?
9. What else could hold more value in terms of happiness for your life?
10. How could you change to be happier? How would you go about making those changes?

3: The Happiness Factor and Change

_____
_____
_____
_____
_____
_____
_____
_____
_____
_____
_____
_____
_____
_____

Happiness and Change

The saying: "Change is as good as a holiday" is very true. Sometimes you do not see you are in a rut – you feel unhappy and don't know why. It could be that your life has become a little mundane. In this case, changing something can be very good 'medicine'.

Often as a life coach, people come to see me because they are feeling unhappy or dissatisfied with their life. They cannot always point out what exactly is causing this feeling. However, once we look at where they are and where they want to be, change is often what is needed. Sometimes this involves my client to leave or change their job or start their own business which may be more aligned with their values. It could be that the environment they are living in is not where they want to be.

The Full Circle

In the area of relationships, this can certainly be massive. Once we explore how they see their relationship, decisions can be made with respect to making adjustments to improve. Often, I hear of individuals who are very unhappy in their relationships but feel powerless to alter this. They stay in this less than ideal situation because they fear the unknown. I have had clients who will say that what they have is better than nothing – better than being alone. I know how that feels since I had the same thoughts, but is "better than nothing" the way? Can't there be more? Can't this be turned around?

Can you imagine for a moment that everything in your life is going along smoothly? You love who you are, where you are in life and who you are sharing your life with. If this was the case, then there would be no need for you to change or look for a new partner. As mentioned previously, self-love is taking responsibility for your actions and your life. Your life is going well because you are taking control. Conversely, if anything should change in your life, for example, if your job is no longer providing you with what you need or want, or your relationship sours, you will handle this much better because you have a high self-esteem. You would take measures to change that which you were unhappy with and not have the attitude that what you have is better than no job or being alone.

> **Write down your first and natural reaction when someone mentions *change***

_____

_____

_____

Take into account though, that you can only alter *yourself*. When it comes to making change, you cannot expect the other person, place

3: The Happiness Factor and Change

or job to make things right. I did not think about this in my past life. I always thought that once "this thing" happened, "that thing" would be better. "If I have this or that, I will be happier."

In my first marriage, we experienced a period of difficulty because my husband had to move to a different town for his work. I was of the opinion that everything would be better if we got to live together again and start a family. Unfortunately, that did not happen because eventually I discovered that children were not in his plan. I stayed with him with the hope that he would change his mind because I didn't think I could change my mind on this. But, as mentioned later in this book, I did change in order to have what I wanted in my life.

In my second marriage, I did not leave when I was unhappy. I hoped that once the children matured, things would be different. I hoped that once the business was better and more profitable, our finances would improve. Once we had better staff, we would have fewer problems. Or once we had our own home, I would be happier. When situations had not eventuated as I had predicted, I was disappointed and unhappy. Past clients and some of my friends have related the same sorts of thoughts and feelings as I had. Fortunately, I have come to understand that if change is to occur, it has to start with and/or from me. I have to change a behaviour or situation.

> *"I am in control of my own happiness, no one else's. I will not change unless I love myself and value my place on this earth."*
>
> **– Paulette Archer**

The wonderful knock on effect to happiness is that if I am happy, it rubs off onto others. Happiness can be infectious. In an attempt to encourage happiness, we are often told that it takes more muscles to frown than to smile. This notion however, does not have any scientific backup. It came about in order to elicit a happier response

The Full Circle

in someone displaying a frown. As human beings, we tend to want everyone around us to be happy. If you know you are in control of your own happiness, then you can choose to be that way. As Aristotle said, "happiness depends on ourselves". This is not a new concept.

Change does not always bring happiness. When I was a child and we moved, the change instead, brought unhappiness at first. I was in a new place and it all seemed so alien to me. Despite this, as things became more familiar with time, I was very happy to be someplace where I could learn new things, meet new people and enjoy new experiences. Reflecting, I know in the end this change made me very happy.

Change and your reactions to it

1. Have you ever had a big change forced on you by outside circumstances? How did you feel? What was your first reaction to the change?

2. After some time, did you feel differently about the change you had to make? Was this change for better or worse?

3. Have you ever been excited about the prospect of change?

4. How were your expectations fulfilled? Were you as happy as expected after the change? Why or why not?

_____

_____

_____

_____

_____

_____

3: The Happiness Factor and Change

Is It You or Change that Brings Happiness?

If happiness is about you and your choices, how come some people are just naturally happier than others? Could it be as a result of their personality, experience, circumstances or other factors? How you view change can be a combination of factors including personality and experiences. It certainly can impact how happy you are about the change. Change can be frightening because of your fears: of failure, of the unknown, of being alone or of making the wrong decisions. However, no fear is worse than staying in a situation which is destructive and disconsolate.

As an example, for someone who is shy, reserved and weary of change, any alteration in their environment and living situation could lead to feelings of isolation or fear. This could be compounded by an inability to assimilate, because everything is so different to what was previously known. Fear of being accepted or understood could lead that person to not taking any steps to get to know others. This could then lead to further isolation and unhappiness.

I am fairly outgoing so I do not usually feel uncomfortable when I'm in a situation where I might not know any or many people. This is quite a contrast to how I felt as a child when I was changing schools and moving countries. Then I felt scared of the unknown and became vulnerable. I did not know what to expect out of any situations I came across, and I often felt lonely. When I was in a new country where I had to learn the language and become familiar with the customs which were alien to me, I felt lost and helpless. When I was in boarding school, I had no family near me so that comfort was missing. Any time I have moved during my life I had the choice to love it or not. Fortunately, largely due to my mother's positive influence earlier in my life, I have always loved it!

There was one time I had moved to an area where many of the residents were involved in the government or military. Because of this they were usually transferred regularly – at least once every two years, sometimes more often. I made a comment once to a woman I met concerning her moves and all the wonderful people she could meet. From my perspective, she was experiencing life in so many new ways. My remark was met with a blank look. It turned out she hated uprooting and moving so often. Her reasons were that she never really got to know people well or make friends because she knew she would be leaving soon and could not stand leaving behind the relationships. As a result, she kept to herself and basically stayed at home with her family. I was amazed that an individual could have so little interest in the people and the world around them.

What this experience taught me, is that we all think differently about everything – including change. For this lady, her perception may have been something which developed over the years as a way to cope with moving time and again. Perhaps her experience of having to leave friends behind was too traumatic for her, so she had chosen not to build relationships at all. Maybe this reaction was a result of her personality. She may have been so shy and reserved that making new friends was very difficult for her. It could also have been experiences from her upbringing that created that mindset.

For many people, change is daunting as it involves a sense of the unknown. You can never actually know a person's motivations for dealing with change or how they react to various circumstances in their lives, unless you learn more about them. What is more important is not passing judgment and being able to accept them for who they are without expecting them to be like you.

3: The Happiness Factor and Change

Your happiness level, friendships and change

1. On a scale of 1-10, how do you rate yourself in terms of being a naturally happy person?

2. What is the reason for the rating you chose? Would you like to be happier? Do you think you can possibly be happier? What would you have to do to alter this?

3. How easily do you make new friends? What makes this easy or hard for you?

4. How comfortable are you in a foreign environment where you may not know many people?

5. Do you interact better in a large or small group environment?

6. How much does your upbringing or personality influence how you interact with new people?

7. How much does the fear of the unknown or change hold you back from experiencing something new?

_____
_____
_____
_____
_____
_____
_____
_____
_____
_____

The Full Circle

My attitude to change has to do with both my personality and my experiences. I have found that most times change has been positive for me. But it can be easier to be comfortable and to stay in your comfort zone. Change can cause discomfort. It may be difficult to adjust to a new way of undertaking an action. More so, when you are familiar with what you are doing in life it seems effective and we are content, we may see no need to change.

I am sure most of you have heard the saying, "if it ain't broke, don't fix it"? If change is imposed on you, it may cause feelings of stress and misery. This could happen if you lose your job, get ill or your relationship breaks down. Once my marriage ended for instance, it took a while for me to adjust to this change in my life. Even though I knew it was for the best, initially I thought I would not survive it on my own. Everything was so different.

Since it wasn't my decision to end the second marriage I did have a choice at least to choose how I reacted to it. In the beginning I struggled because I had not been on my own for many years. I felt lost and empty. I felt lonely and frightened. I felt betrayed and abandoned. Were these some of the feelings I had as a child when the family moved or when I was placed in boarding school? I believe so; however, it wasn't until I started working on myself that the connection was made again.

When my older daughter was two, we moved to a very small town out west in country Queensland, Australia. We had to because of our business. This was not in the "original" plan. I looked forward to it hoping it would make a difference in our lives and I looked forward to that change because it was an adventure. It was an opportunity for me to be in a new place and experience a completely different way of life. We had moved to an area that was new to my husband, daughter and me and it was up to us, not the outside influences, whether to be happy or not. I made friends easily due to the nature of the environment and have many excellent memories from my time there. To be candid, it was one of the happiest times in my married life.

By contrast, much later in life, being on my own did not seem like something I would be happy with. Contentment, or any level of happiness, was very far from my mind at that point. From living through my life story, I believe many of you will be experiencing this as well. You may find yourself in situations where you know being on your own is far preferable to what you are experiencing in your relationship or living or working environment. However, you feel powerless to do anything. Fear of the unknown can be crippling.

From my upbringing I learnt to accept change somewhat reluctantly to begin with. Nonetheless, with no other choice at the time, it was done willingly. I have seen situations where children can make a move very hard on the parents, due to their extreme unhappiness regarding decisions they made. These are times when parents need to make decisions which can cause displeasure within the family and there is always the possibility that someone will not be happy with the choice. I was fortunate to have parents who were the type of people who saw change as a "gift". Hence, my sister and I were always encouraged to enjoy all that came our way.

When we did make our next move or travel to a new place, we learnt to look forward to it and embrace it. (Mind you, it was not always easy and it was something I did struggle with as a child.) Fortunately, this outlook did give me a thirst for knowledge about other lands, cultures and the people who live there. Each relocation became another great experience.

Would I have been the same if I had not had these experiences? I can't say for sure, but I do firmly believe that my experiences helped form my attitude regarding change. This being that it can be difficult, however, I know ultimately that I will adjust and perhaps be in a much better position. Change has also meant I am experiencing something I may not have encountered if this had not occurred. As you get into your later years, change may be more difficult to adapt to. You may be more set in your habits, environment and ways. I see people who once embraced change with adventurous abandon, now being a little more resistant to it.

This resistance can be increased due to the fact that, as you age, your cognitive functions can be affected – your attention and memory, as well as physical alterations due to hearing or visual loss, or changes in the brain or other parts of your body. Because of this, you hold onto what you know best rather than shifting as you may have done in the past.

Change was hard for me in my first years after my second divorce. It was that way because I had lost my self-esteem and did not believe I was capable of being on my own. I was not prepared for and had not expected such a change. I sometimes wonder as I age if I will become resistant to change? I guess I'll have to wait and see what happens when I am "old" – whatever "old" is! I am hoping that my passion for learning will carry me through so that I never give up embracing or accepting change in my life.

You Mean I Can Choose to Be Happy?

Being happy is definitely a choice. It is true that there are many circumstances in your life that are beyond your control – like rain on your wedding day. But you can choose to be happy because it is your wedding day, regardless of the rain. You cannot stop the rain, but you can carry on with your celebrations.

For many of you, your response to change is influenced by your attitudes and beliefs. Your attitudes are your perception of something and your beliefs are your own opinions about it. Your values tend to stem from your beliefs. Exemplifying once again with rain on your wedding day, one response could be to get angry, upset and extremely unhappy about it. This could then lead to you having a bad day because of it. Another response could be to turn things around and take the tack that "it's good luck when it rains on your wedding day".

In believing everything happens for a reason, I always try to the best of my capacity to turn negatives into positives. An horrendous situation occurred to a family member of a friend of mine. As bad as it was, she has turned the situation into something positive, choosing to be happy. Based on what we know about our beliefs and attitudes, in this example, my friend's belief was to turn this otherwise tragic situation into a more positive one so she would not be heartbroken by the experience. Her values around this may have been strength, which meant she was better able to accept what had happened. Or perhaps love, family and commitment motivated her reactions, which may have been the case in the following example.

A close friend of mine had a son who was diagnosed with severe Autism and medical problems. Her husband left her and she became the sole parent of this gorgeous boy. I could perceive how this could have led to unhappiness, despair or giving up. None of this happened as she remains one of the happiest people I have ever met.

Of course, caring for her son can be challenging at times, but she did not waste time thinking about the negatives from the very beginning. Instead, she took that situation and turned it into something positive. She started a lifelong mission to advocate for Autism and continues to do everything possible to help her son, and many others like him, in order to have the best life possible. Her approach will, hopefully, lead to some independence for her son as he reaches adulthood. She had a choice with regard to her situation and her choice was to be happy in spite of the cards she was dealt. On account of her passion to help her son, she has been instrumental in helping many others in quite similar circumstances.

Similarly, there are situations in which I make conscious decisions to be happy. My choice is aligned with whether or not I am being accountable for my actions and live 'at cause' rather than 'at effect'.

The Full Circle

I will be going into more detail about this concept in the next chapter. For now, being 'at cause' means to take full *responsibility* for whatever part *you* play in your life. On the other hand, being 'at effect' means to take on the victim role and pass the *blame* on to everyone or everything that happens to you. When you are at cause you decide on your own happiness and do not let outside events control you. If I am living at cause, I will not let my circumstances decide my happiness. Although there are times that I go into victim mode, even now, the norm is that I do take control and I choose to be happy.

It would be understandable if parents become the victim when faced with the circumstances of an autistic child. Friends and family may even expect the family involved to be devastated and reluctant to accept the situation. Their friends and family may feel sorry for them and let them stay in their victim mode agreeing with comments like "why me!", "we'll never cope!" or "it's not fair". My friend could have been crestfallen and no one would have blamed her for the way she felt. With an unwell child and a husband deserting her in her biggest time of need, most would have expected her – and accepted her – if she became a "victim". Instead, she chose to live at cause. She chose happiness for herself and her son.

> *"You may think you need a pity party sometimes, but happiness parties are way better! Bring more of those into your life and be grateful for them."*
> **– Paulette Archer**

There are bound to be times in your life where you have that 'pity party' which might sometimes be okay. Being strong all the time may not be possible. Just do not linger too long in that emotional space. How often have you spoken to someone who is always complaining? It always seems as though the world is against them and that nothing good ever happens to them. That is an example of someone who is living at effect – blaming everyone and everything else for their unhappiness or thinking it is just plain bad luck.

> **Your happiness and choice**
>
> 1. Do you believe happiness is a choice or something that 'just happens'?
> 2. Have you had any experiences in your life where you chose to be happy despite your circumstances? What were they? How did they make you feel?
> 3. Looking back, have there been situations in your life where you think the outcome could have been better or different if you had made a conscious choice to be happy?

_____

_____

_____

_____

_____

_____

By changing your thinking, you can change your circumstances in your life. According to **Buddha**, *"We are what we think. All that we are arises with our thoughts. With our thoughts, we make the world."* This is not a new concept.

If this is true, it means that happiness has more to do with adaptation than our circumstances. I believe that adaptation is normal. By this I mean that you tend to react to situations with an alteration in your emotions – your happiness level. You then go back, or adapt back, to your baseline level of happiness. Over time, that baseline level can fluctuate. Positive adaptation comes about when you are faced with a negative situation and how you use coping mechanisms to deal with that adversity in a positive way. You adapt to this negative situation, rather than fixing it. You choose to exhibit the right attitude despite the tides. This is how my friend managed her life living and caring for her autistic son.

> *"Everything in your life is a reflection of a choice you have made.*
> *If you want a different result, make a different choice."*
> **– Unknown**

I like the saying "variety is the spice of life". Change is a huge factor here. Whatever the circumstances are, they can transform you. Still, it is your reaction that really decides your happiness. You can choose how you react to the change. If you take in the concept of adaptation, you can continue at this level of happiness until another situation occurs that impacts you. If you maintain a certain level of happiness throughout your life, you can simply adapt and never seek anything more. Alternatively, you may have adapted to those situations so much that now you are not as happy with this circumstance as you were previously.

Take into consideration romantic relationships. At the beginning there is the fire and passion that keeps you on a high note. Then, perhaps life settles into a routine which can often be construed as mundane. Boredom with this routine can change your attitude and behaviour toward your partner. As a result, a person's happiness levels drop. The unhappy person starts to want more or expect changes in the relationship. This would be the time to look at what is happening in the relationship to see what can be done to get the passion back.

For some this isn't necessary. The couple is happy with the way things are and change is not needed. For others no dialogue is initiated, instead blame is levied on one person. This can lead to the demise of the relationship. In some cases, this could even lead to abuse. The person who no longer feels happy is looking for someone to blame and acts out on their partner. In this way they do not have to take any responsibility for their lack of happiness – they believe it is the other person's fault.

Ironically, often times when you most need a positive approach to change and adaptation you are in the least positive mindset. In the low times it becomes easier to blame or become the victim. In my experience, when I was feeling down I was more likely to blame or be the victim. At this time, I was in a negative frame of mind and would forget the good things I had in my life. I would become so fixated with the problem as I saw it, that the "problem" became the only thing which existed in my life at that time.

I would enter a dark space where nothing rational or positive would be evident. It would be as if someone had taken my mind and erased every good memory and replaced it with a black hole of misery. At times the negativity was so bad that no amount of convincing could make me feel otherwise. This is being in serious victim mode. I was totally at effect and from experience I can tell you it is not a good place to be. Remember, I was at effect for my part alone – no one else's.

Fortunately, in my life now, those moments do not exist anymore. If I feel a bit low occasionally, I am able to recognise it, acknowledge it and let it go. For many years I had chronic tension headaches and severe pain and other symptoms of IBS (irritable bowel syndrome). At that time, I frequently took medication which did not always help. I was often debilitated for days at a time. I did not cope well and this circle of pain and depression continued. Although I do have chronic back pain, which occurred post-divorce when I injured my back while moving house, I rarely use pain medication and cope well. I subsequently have had four back surgeries and suffered nerve damage along with certain other mobility issues. Now however, I have various methods of treating my chronic pain. I control it – the pain does not control me.

My attitude towards the pain is different and I do not feel like the victim any more. I can look at what I have, not what I don't. I keep myself busy and often immerse myself in activities to redirect my focus. I rest when I need to because I am aware that it is necessary for repair and rejuvenation, as I tend to overdo it at times. Now, when I rest, I no longer feel lazy or useless – which was something I often felt in the past. My attitude towards this was twofold. My mother was always busy working in and around the house. I never saw her sitting around at home. I decided that this is how it was meant to be if you are a wife and mother.

To add to this, later in life it did not help when I was questioned about what I had done during the day by my husband. I felt as if I had to report about my very busy day doing what needed to be done without any hint of relaxation. I did not want to be blamed for being lazy. I believed I had to justify my position at all times. Of course, these were some of the reasons I was unhappy and discontented with my life.

Also, in the past, my happiness was affected when I felt low, yet, I put on the face of someone who is happy so as not to 'rock the boat' or, so I would not have to own my feelings. I often felt that there was nothing I could do about the way I felt, so I just existed. I appeared happy on the outside but was really disheartened on the inside. The worst was that I felt totally incapable of doing anything about it. Now, I admit that when my life is not in alignment with my values, it can lead to a low time for me.

For a number of years, I lost sight of my own values and that led to a high degree of despondency. There were times that I wanted to avoid life by going to bed and sleeping, thinking that if I was asleep, I would not be aware. Of course, when I woke up, the low was still lurking around. Alternatively, I might have gone out to avoid home and everything associated with it. Naturally, when I returned home, it was all still there, so that does not solve anything either.

When I suffered the most with IBS and chronic tension headaches, I was at my lowest emotionally. These issues were at their worst from the age of about 34 to 54. Naturally, this would affect my happiness because, physically, I was not well and could only feel the negative spiraling effect of the medical issues. I was on a constant circle of pain and misery. After my second divorce, my life began to change because of the self-development work I was doing. I became empowered and those problems disappeared. Taking measures to be at cause leads to empowerment and can resolve so many issues in your life.

Happiness, Attitude and Gratitude

> *"Gratitude unlocks the fullness of life. It turns what we have into enough, and more.*
> *It turns denial into acceptance, chaos to order, confusion to clarity.*
> *It can turn a meal into a feast, a house into a home, a stranger into a friend."*
> **– Melody Beattie**

I am grateful for all of the happiest moments in my life which hold great value for me. Many of these times were spent with family or close friends, which forms one of my core values. As far back as I remember while I was a child, the family always went to my maternal grandparents' home for holidays when possible. These occasions were infrequent because they lived in another state and, of course, we moved away from the U.S. Regardless, I have such wonderful memories of these visits.

The Full Circle

Apart from time with my grandparents, I had many other relatives nearby so I could play with all of my cousins. I loved my grandma's cooking. She would bake and make all sorts of little treats for me and I was given some things I was not allowed at home – specifically, drinking coffee! My grandparents worked in the local movie theatre. My grandma ran the ticket office and popcorn stand and my grandpa ran the projector. As a child, I felt very important since I got free popcorn and I could go up into the projection room and watch while the movie was being run. Whenever I go to the movies, I am always reminded of them – especially when I smell popcorn!

Close friends of my family, who later became my guardians when I was living in the U.S. while my parents were in South America, also gave me some wonderful memories that I will never forget. I feel gratitude even now when I ponder those days. Before my family first relocated overseas, we spent many a day or evening with this family. All of us children would play together while our parents played cards, and in the evenings, everyone would gather around the piano for a bit of a sing-along.

Christmas always brought many incredibly memorable times, as it was a very family-oriented time for me. As a child, I loved Christmas Eve when 'Santa' would come. Even now, my daughters still want Santa to come since they want to recreate those happy memories from their childhood. With or without Santa, Christmas is a special time and brings much jubilation to me. I am still grateful for being able to share this time with family and friends. Going skiing together with my children were outstanding times. The family would be out of the regular swing of things – normal life, so to speak – and all the cares and worries were not present for our time away doing what we all loved.

Other times which hold euphoric memories in alignment with my values are accomplishments in my education, or the education of those I love and am close to. I remember as a child when my father attained his Master's degree. Perhaps this is where my values around education stemmed.

At the time, I was young so I barely understood the significance of the actual degree. But I knew enough to know that it was a very important achievement for him and we all celebrated. Akin to that, when I achieved my degree and when my daughters achieved theirs, those times were magic moments. It is not hard for me to feel grateful for the opportunity to further my education and for the ability to help my daughters earn degrees.

I often have drawn strength from momentous occasions when I have been low and reminded myself that my life is not static. My attitude around those memories is happiness and pleasure. Although there were many times I was in despair, I could grasp onto the good and enjoyable times in the hope it would always be that way, yet knowing for me, the unhappiness may return.

Now my experiences are altered, but no less important. I have built a new life for myself and it is outstanding. I do not have my life as it was, but that is okay. As I grow and change, I can take the best parts and expand them to have a happier and more desirable life today. It is how my attitude to life is now compared to a decade or so ago, and once again, I can choose to be happy.

Can you draw on those times from your past that were especially wonderful? Times when you experienced untold happiness and know that if it was possible once, you can surely get it back? If you cannot think of times in your life that were fantastic with untold happiness, perhaps revisit Chapter 1. Pay particular note in regard to self-love and then go through the special highlighted questions you have answered so far. Perhaps you might reconsider that there may have been some wonderful times in your life, but perhaps those times are hidden due to the way you may be feeling at present.

The Full Circle

Happiness comes from within. Once we are contented within ourselves, we aren't necessarily looking for more that will make us happy. If your happiness is too self-centered, you can easily become dispirited because you may be looking for a bigger, brighter, newer, faster and best of everything. If you are always wanting the latest gadget, new 'toy' or new partner because you have become unhappy with the old, I would think that happiness would be much harder to achieve.

Remember when we talked about the Four Levels of Happiness at the beginning of the Chapter? We saw in Level 2 which is more comparative, that this has to do with personal achievement and ego-gratification. If you are totally focused on yourself, then possibly you will never be truly happy if all of your happiness comes from external means rather than from within.

When I immerse myself in helping others for instance or engage in some activity which can take all the focus from me, I notice that I am exhilarated. I feel grateful that I can give to others in need or less fortunate. As mentioned, for a large part of my life, I have taken on volunteer work which I continue to do.

Growing up both as a child and as an adult, I witnessed my parents participating in volunteer work. As a matter of fact, my father was still doing volunteer work at the age of 90! Volunteering gives me a great deal of satisfaction and joy. This is aligned with Happiness Level 3. You experience happiness in different ways, which has to do with your own expectations, values and experiences. If happiness is truly within you, it just has to surface when the situation arises. Your attitude towards it is seen by your actions.

My happiness is not about how much I can have for myself, but more about what I can do to help others in their lives. I get the biggest buzz helping others achieve contentment for themselves, this, in turn, delights me. I have done some pro bono work in my coaching business and find the personal reward for this is tremendous. I have a lot to be thankful for and I love to be able to give back.

Happiness comes when I learn more about the way I think, as well as the way others think and act. I am also particularly happy when I have an 'ah-ha' moment. An ah-ha moment can be explained as that moment when something has become crystal clear, which I may not have comprehended previously. These are moments when I really see life as it is and have learnt something from a situation that has arisen.

Happiness is linked to my inner peace as opposed to whether or not I have the biggest house, the best car or the most jewelry. When I was at that stage of my life around the 30 to 50 age bracket, I was looking for external means for happiness. I was not happy within myself so I believed all the other 'stuff' was the essence of happiness. Certainly, if you have financial wealth the possibility exists to be able to help more people. However, I have been able to help others without money.

As I have shared in this Chapter, true happiness comes from an inner peace, which I mostly find when I experience gratitude. Gratitude is something many of you perhaps seldom focus on because the world tells us there is always more and we deserve more. While this may be true, it can leave you with a sense of emptiness, never being satisfied with what you have and often taking it all for granted. Yet, when you practice gratitude, when you look around and appreciate all the things and people you have in your life, you no longer feel empty, you can feel full and at peace.

In addition to the answers you provided to questions in your journal, I would like to make another suggestion. Turn your journal into a *gratitude journal* as well. Each time you sit down to work through something, first take the time to write down three things you are grateful for. Write the date next to each entry so you can refer to it later on and remember why you felt gratitude at that time.

The Full Circle

> *"Develop an attitude of gratitude, and give thanks for everything that happens to you, knowing that every step forward is a step toward achieving something bigger and better than your current situation."*
> **– Brian Tracy**

It is easy to be happy in your life if that is what you want. What is your attitude towards your life and your happiness level? Can you see that you can control all of this as long as you take responsibility for your life and the way you operate in it? Do you believe you can take responsibility? Do you want to live at cause? Let's turn over to the next chapter to see how best to do this so you can take the victim mentality out of your life forever.

4: Understanding Living 'At Cause' or 'At Effect'

"Every man builds his world in his own image. He has the power to choose, but not the power to escape the necessity of choice."

– Ayn Rand

Being 'at cause' and 'at effect' is really a powerful language pattern of NLP (Neuro-Linguistic Patterning). This is an approach to communication, personal development and changing your belief systems as well as psychotherapy. I was not aware of the meaning of being 'at cause' or 'at effect' until I started my journey into Personal Development. I definitely did not realise that I had been living a good part of my life mostly at effect – especially in the latter years.

Somehow, I had lost the ability to find solutions to any of my so-called issues. I felt powerless – unable to change how I felt or how I was living. Interestingly enough, at the time, I thought it was normal to feel this way. I had a pretty rough time, and many of the people I communicated with had similar thoughts.

What I felt were hard times may have been completely different from those harsh times many of you had or still have. I can only speak from my experiences or with the people I have worked with or been close to. For any of us though, when a situation is perceived as abhorrent, it does not matter what the situation is, it is tagged horrible.

The Full Circle

Many people live at effect. This is when **you** *blame* people or circumstances for what has gone wrong in **your** life. You may have heard people say such things as "it's the boss's fault", "the company that I work for is terrible", "my wife is a nag", "my husband hasn't got a clue", or even "it's not my fault I'm fat, it's in my genes". In other words, when you live at effect, your life and your happiness will merely be a spin off result from everyone and everything around you. You believe that nothing is your fault but, at the same time, you feel like you cannot do anything to change it. It is no wonder I felt powerless when I was living at effect.

> **Your life and *your* control over it**
> 1. Do you ever feel like life is just happening to you?
> 2. That it is all out of control, especially your control?
> 3. Why do you think you feel this way?

_____
_____
_____
_____
_____

The opposite of being 'at effect' is being 'at cause'. This is one of the most liberating and powerful tools you can apply to your life. Being at cause means that **you** decide what you will do in your life and take *full responsibility* for the part **you** play. It impacts in a very real way on how you live your life. You see the world as a place of opportunity and you take steps to go for what you desire in your life. If you are faced with roadblocks, you change course so that you can find other opportunities to achieve what you desire. You know that you have a choice and that you do not need to react to events or other people's words or actions.

This concept is at the core of personal development. When you are not taking responsibility in your life, you will blame people or events for being unhappy, sick or for having a bad job, etc. It is always someone else's fault or something else that has caused the situation to occur. The basic premise with being at effect is *blame*. When you are at effect you are generally unhappy but think that it is not your fault and you cannot do anything to change. By contrast, if you are in control of your life and happy, then you are at cause. Simplistically, you never have another reason or excuse for feeling powerless. *Accepting responsibility* is the main premise for living at cause.

> *"I like the thought that if there's going to be anyone to blame, it's going to be me."*
> **– Laura Marling**

It can be difficult to live totally at cause, and at times I still go into victim mode. When I was introduced to this concept over a decade ago, I was depressed, on medication and felt worthless. I wanted change more than anything! I was in my mid 50's, separated and at the lowest point in my life. I was working with a counselor who ran group and private sessions. These sessions consisted of intense self-analysis and healing.

The self-analysis looked at understanding my personality, emotions and behaviour so that I could heal. The sessions also gave me my first exposure to the concept of being at cause or at effect. This concept was quite difficult for me to grasp at the beginning. It seemed to me that being 'at cause' meant that I was the only one who was responsible for the negative occurrences in my life. However, that is not the case. It is about taking responsibility only for *my* part in each situation. I had control over what I did or said, not what anyone else did or said.

In addition to the counseling, I started my training to become a Life Coach. This training had quite a bit of self-analysis as well. Along with my coaching training, I studied to become a volunteer crisis counselor. Once again, in all of these courses and training I spent a great deal of time looking within myself. Being able to know for yourself what it is that motivates and drives you also helps in knowing others. This is important if you are going to be working with people and assisting them to make change in their life.

As I was learning more about myself, I started to learn to love myself. It was not until I trained in NLP that I started seeing the big picture and really began to understand more fully the concept of being at cause or at effect. Without understanding this concept and bringing it into my life, I do not believe the change in me would have been as effective as it has been.

Traditional counseling, psychology and psychiatry – all of which I have experienced – does not seem to mention cause and effect in the same way as with the NLP training. And, these traditional methods usually take longer before you see results. When I started my NLP training, my healing evolved quite rapidly. This is because I was looking at my life differently. It had an immense impact on my life. Once I truly grasped the concept, it was life changing. Now I have no need to think events occurring in my life are someone else's fault. I can own my problems and any difficulties that arise. I always have a choice and can make all the decisions for myself that I need. Of course, I always had this at my disposal. It was just that my eyes had never been open to this possibility before.

It is shocking to realise I had spent so many years believing I had no choice. Now I know this simply is not true. You always have a

4: Understanding Living 'At Cause' or 'At Effect'

choice. I am just like many of you who have experienced some challenges. There are many people who have been in that space of feeling powerless. This is one of the reasons I wanted to write this book. I would like to share with you also if you think as I did, that you have no choice. Rest assured change *is* possible. You do have a choice. By really understanding the concept of being at cause or at effect, it is possible to be free of self-limiting beliefs, which is extremely damaging and can cause you to lose your self-esteem.

The Full Circle

> **Think about whether or not you have been living 'at cause' or 'at effect'**
>
> Take some time to do this. **Write down your answers in your journal.**
>
> 1. Consider the past years of your life. Have any events happened that turned your world upside down? Think about what they were and write down a description of each event.
>
> 2. In your mind, what caused those events to occur? Was it other people? Was it the environment you were in? Was it the people you were surrounded by? Was it the economy? The company? The industry? Write down a list of everyone and everything you think were to blame for the occurrence.
>
> 3. How did you react to the events? What was your emotional reaction? What was your physical reaction? What did you do?
>
> 4. Did you ever feel like you were a victim – like you had no control over what was happening to you?
>
> 5. What was the outcome of the events? Were there positive or negative outcomes? Why do you feel they were positive or negative?
>
> 6. Looking back now, do you think there is anything you could have done to change the events or the outcome of the events? If so, what would you have done if you were to relive them? Alternatively, can you see that if you were not able to change the event, you could have changed your reaction to it?
>
> 7. And now, if you are still 'at effect', can you see that being this way served you at the time and gave you the chance to deny responsibility and, therefore, deny any part you had to play? Is it possible you blamed someone else?

4: Understanding Living 'At Cause' or 'At Effect'

How Much Fun is Living 'At Effect'?

When you live at effect, it really is about someone or something else causing your problem. A few examples of this could be: I am fat because my body metabolises slowly (not because I eat too much and do not exercise). If my husband loved me, we would be happy (not what part do I play in our unhappiness). If my boss understood me, I would do much better (not perhaps I could speak with my boss to see what sort of solutions we could come up with). Or, when the children are older, life will be better (not let's find out how I can make things better now).

This is a victim mentality which reflects how you are thinking about your life and impacts your daily experiences. It can also have consequences on the larger life issues.

For instance, thoughts such as: "If he hadn't done that to me just before the job interview, I would have gotten the position." This is just shifting blame to someone else. If the job was that important and was something you wanted that badly, you would suck up what you were feeling, put on a brave face and ace the interview. Another example could be: "I flunked my exam because there were too many outside noises and I could not concentrate." There will always be outside noise in life and it usually happens at the most inconvenient times. Make a plan, even if it means stuffing tissues in your ears. Is the exam important? Do you need the pass? Then get on with it and write it. You have one opportunity to do so. Do whatever you have to do to get through it!

At different times in my life there are examples that stand out. One in particular, was when I was nursing. I had been working a number of years in a job in which I was not very happy. Much had changed since I began there. I lived an hour away and the commute put two more hours into my work day. I had tried to find other jobs which would have been closer to where I lived, but had been unsuccessful, so I stayed even though I was unhappy.

The Full Circle

During my time at this job, there had been many changes within the company that the employees were unhappy with. The atmosphere was not very positive. All these reasons, of course, were perfect for me to place blame! I allowed these to take an emotional toll on me. In reality, no one has control over my emotions but me. However, I let certain situations influence my perception.

One of the reasons I stayed was because it was in my comfort zone and going out of that to face change, was daunting. If I quit without having another job to go to, I thought I may not be able to manage. How hard did I look for another job, knowing that I may not be happy in this job but a new one is unknown, and what if it was worse? I did not take responsibility for my life at that time and I decided my job was to blame for my unhappiness. This was definitely me living at effect. Once I started being at cause I made the decision to leave. It was not surprising that I got another job and realised how much my negativity and blame shifting had controlled me.

> *"Playing the victim can be a dreadful existence - don't go there!"*
> **– Paulette Archer**

Many a time, it can feel like the whole world is against you! It is as if each step you take forward is alternated by two steps backwards, thereby never making any progress.

So, how would you know if you were living 'at effect'?

Here is a simple test to take to see how you stack up in this area:

- Is life always getting in the way of your dreams?
- Do you often find out that negative occurrences always happen to you?
- Is your life a soap opera of calamity and drama?

4: Understanding Living 'At Cause' or 'At Effect'

- Do you sometimes feel no matter how hard you try, things just do not change?
- Do you feel if you were given this opportunity or chance, things would be fine? Except you never have that opportunity, so you never had a chance.

If you answered *yes* to any or all of these questions, you are living 'at effect' and the circle of this pattern has been set.

But now, it is time to change. Without change, you will find many repercussions remaining with this frame of mind. There will be way more negative occurrences than positive ones. There will always be a valid reason for bad things happening. You will live a life of excuses and will not live up to your full potential. If you believe there is nothing you can do about any situation or the way others treat you, you are more likely to stay in situations that are less than ideal. This is simply because you believe it is not your fault. Things will tend to just happen – you do not make any choice about what transpires, and you can just play the victim.

Since we all have moments like this, it is a question of whether this victim mentality is the exception or the norm. If there seems to be no likelihood of other solutions, possibilities or outcomes, you may think: "this is the way it is and that's life". "Life is hard and I just have to put up with it". This line of thinking will cause hopeless and helpless feelings and attitudes you cannot do anything about. Sometimes you even feel your life is worthless or your hands are tied!

All of these can potentially lead you to suffer from physical maladies as they induce stress and anxiety into one's life. Concentration and focus on your life may be diminished. The default when something does not go to plan is to blame someone or something else.

Studies have shown that people who grow up in poorer communities are more likely to remain poor, despite opportunities that are presented to them. This is because they live in the mindset of being at effect. These individuals may feel powerless to change their circumstances. Robert Kiyosaki talks about this in his well-known book *Rich Dad, Poor Dad*. The book discusses how mindset can impact success.

Still, rules get broken. There are enough rags to riches stories to prove it. Ben Carson, born in 1951 in inner city Detroit, was an American doctor who overcame poverty, failing grades in junior school, racism and a violent temper to become a world-renowned neurosurgeon. Oprah Winfrey is a well-known celebrity who was born to a single teenage mother who lived in poverty. During her childhood, she sustained considerable hardship, was raped at the age of nine and had a baby at 14. Nothing in this world seems to have stopped her from achieving greatness. (These people, by the way, live 'at cause' – they learnt to take responsibility.)

These stories may have moved you, but you think "My life isn't like that so I can't be living at effect". Keep in mind, there are just as many people in first world countries not living in poverty who are living at effect. It is not about how wealthy or successful you are, it is about being in control in your life.

> *"Life is not a matter of chance it is a matter of choice. It is not something to be waited for it is something to be achieved."*
> **– Unknown**

Switching Gears: Living 'At Cause'

The majority of people I encounter who stay at effect do so because this is where they feel comfortable. Even though they may not feel as happy as they could, they do not know how to change or think it is even possible. If this is you, you may not feel comfortable stretching yourself because it can be frightening and take you out of your comfort zone. It then becomes easier to accept things as they are, rather than trying something new. The circle of your life here, like mine, just goes round and round – no beginning and no end. No change and no possibility of change, or so you believe.

> **Staying in your comfort zone**
>
> Even if it is not the life you want, does the thought of change frighten you enough to make you stay exactly where you are, even though you may know it is not the best for you?

_____

_____

_____

_____

Many of my clients have come to me with these thoughts of it being easier to stay where they are than to change because of fear of the unknown. They realise they are unhappy but do not always understand why or where it is coming from.

If you live this way, you may also do so because you are responding to other people's emotional states (the way those people live and think about their lives). You have become used to agreeing with everyone else rather than making decisions for yourself. You may want to follow the leader and not be the leader. Perhaps your own self-esteem is such that your self-limiting beliefs paralyse you. You do not want to 'rock the boat' by not agreeing with someone because you might get told off that your ideas are useless.

If you decide that you want more, you might come up against doubters who you allow to talk you out of something, because they believe change is not possible. As a result, you may be happy to settle for less and stay in your comfort zone, using all the excuses possible for why your situation is different from others and remains unchanged. What can happen to you is that you may be living day to day without your own goals and dreams fulfilled, which then can lead to a certain amount of unhappiness. You do not always recognise it though. Daily, you may talk to people who have similar challenges. Those individuals seem "normal" so you continue down the same path without making any changes.

"If you are at effect then it's a good chance the people around you are there also. Don't take on other's thoughts and attitudes so you fit into the mould. Be your own person, take responsibility, leave the group and begin living at cause."
– Paulette Archer

I have met many people over the years who have said they were unhappy in their lives, in their marriage or in their jobs. Yet, few of them were willing to do anything about altering their life. For me, I had a dreamlike "hope" that somehow things would be different. When I was at my lowest, I hoped everyone else would get better. I did not realise I had the power to change and be different. I stayed like I was because it seemed comfortable and normal.

My husband and I were not getting along, the children were causing difficulties, I was alone longing for my family back in the U.S., finances were tenuous, staff was dishonest – and so it went. There was always something or someone else causing my unhappiness.

After I started crisis counseling and Life Coaching, I saw that many people were incapable of moving from the place of despair and inability to change, just as I had. They did not know how and they were afraid to try. Fear is a big stopper preventing us from moving forward. When I became single again in my 50's, I also felt petrified. I really had not spent much time on my own and honestly believed I couldn't. I had no faith in my abilities and I had a very low self-esteem.

4: Understanding Living 'At Cause' or 'At Effect'

I went into a deep depression, lost a lot of weight and had moments when I simply did not want to live. I could empathise with many of my clients during my crisis counseling days – I had been in the same place as they were only a short time before.

Nonetheless, out of that very low place, I became aware this was not where I wanted to stay. I quickly took steps to change. I was almost in a frenzy to get as much help as quickly as I could so that I could feel better immediately. I did not like the way it affected me and I am certain, for any of you who have been in a similar situation, you will agree. Totally losing your power means, YOU DO NOT FEEL GOOD!

Unfortunately, many of us just stay there and get deeper into the victim mode. I cannot say I changed immediately. There was a certain amount of grieving that had not occurred. For any of us who has had a loss, no matter what that loss is, grieving needs to be acknowledged. It is okay to grieve and it is necessary in order to return to an enhanced self-esteem.

Grief is a natural response to loss, whether it is from negative occurrences such as death of a close person or pet, divorce or relationship breakdown, loss of a job, financial insecurity, health or trauma. The grieving process was first proposed by Elisabeth Kübler-Ross in her 1969 book *On Death and Dying*. Although she researched individuals facing death and dying, grief is now generalised to all types of loss and negative life changes. The five stages of normal grief are: Denial and Isolation, Anger, Bargaining, Depression, and Acceptance. These stages do not necessarily appear in any order and each stage can last varying amounts of time. All stages may not be experienced either.

It is important to acknowledge the grieving process because it is essential for your healing. It does take time and, if it is not resolved, it could lead to more serious problems including complicated grieving, (which means you are stuck in an intense state of mourning), depression and even suicide.

The Revelation of Living a Life 'At Cause'

As already mentioned, being at cause is taking responsibility for everything that happens in your life. You make your own decisions with regard to what you desire. Most importantly, when you *know* you have a choice, you can examine how your decisions affect others; but in no way are you responsible for how **those** individuals react to them.

Interestingly enough, when you are living this way it seems easier to get what you want. It is amazing that when you get into the habit of thinking more positively, the "bad stuff" tends to stop happening. Have you ever heard someone say: "everything fell into place" and they didn't miss a beat while attempting to do "that thing"? This is an example of being at cause. As opposed to those who say "nothing ever goes right for me, bad things happen all the time, I never get a break". I know which category I would like to fall into.

Currently, I am very aware of the concept. I am able to change course and correct my frame of thought quite easily if I slip into the negative. As a coach, I often ask questions targeted at helping my clients discern their way of thinking. Usually I can see it; however, it is important that they see it for themselves. I prompt them to alter a statement which may have been negative and turn it around to the positive. It is remarkable to see what happens when people understand clearly what is possible – that it is okay to go for what they want – and to be in control.

The Power Buzz of Taking Back Control!

When you live at cause, your circle of life will be buzzing with excitement and you will be living a more fulfilled and contented life. There is also the possibility of being more successful in life because you will now be taking action and striving for certain goals and success for yourself.

Because you are more focused on what you want in your life, you are more likely to achieve those things. You will most likely take steps on a regular basis to achieve success and will be striving for more. You will be willing to get out of your comfort zone and do what it takes to accomplish your goals. You are not sitting back waiting for someone else to do things for you.

Individuals who live at cause are people who make things happen. They tend to be happier and are less likely to suffer from extreme stress and depression than those living at effect. This concept is very powerful because it means you surely do have a say in what is happening in your life. You feel completely in control and there is no better feeling than this.

I remember a specific time when I felt completely in control. The individual I was dealing with wanted, instead, to be in control in a power struggle sort of way. Because I had certainty about what I was doing and saying, I was able to stay calm and relaxed and I stood my ground. The other person, however, lost total control and became very frustrated. He started screaming and blaming everyone and everything else. He took no responsibility with respect to the issue at hand or with regard to his part in the situation.

It was appalling to experience at the time. However, I could retain confidence about myself and the outcome. I did not let his response affect how I was going to deal with the situation or feel about it. When I compare how I felt when I was at effect and how I feel now, it is worlds apart. That same situation would have totally crushed me. Now, tough situations are not challenging. Life is astounding and filled with possibility!

The Full Circle

> **Now that you know about living 'at cause' or 'at effect', ask yourself where *you* are at the moment**
>
> 1. Refer to the events you listed in your journal when you considered the past years of your life a few pages back. For each one, write down if you surmise your response was being at effect or at cause?
>
> 2. Looking back, if there were events in which you think you were at effect, were there any situations you could have taken responsibility for? Write down what you believe you could have done and how you suppose it could have influenced the outcomes?
>
> 3. Is there anything you could do right now that would change how you think or feel about the events that came about? What would you do? How would it change the outcome or how you feel about what eventuated?

When you begin to acknowledge just how easy it is to take responsibility for your life, you will find that you feel liberated. It may have been a while since you lost control over your life, like I did. You may feel as if you have really hit rock bottom and there is no hope. You may be totally crushed right now, but are you broken? The answer is no. You may be crushed but you are not broken, neither am I.

5: Crushed But Not Broken

"If we will be quiet and ready enough, we shall find compensation in every disappointment."
– Henry David Thoreau

I remember the day my husband told me he was leaving me. It was effectively the worst day of my life. I was crushed, broken and in utter despair. The thoughts raging through my mind were: "How could this happen?"; "How did I let it happen?"; "What had I done wrong?" My first reaction was despair. Then it turned into anger, then fear. How could he do this? He had promised me a lifetime together. But then again, he had promised me many things. I had made promises too, and both of us had broken them. If I was honest with myself, I had been living in a private hell for some time in my marriage. When I was hurt, I lashed back, hoping to inflict as much pain in return. I was angry and scared. But I would not admit it to myself, and certainly not to anyone else.

I had to keep up the everything's fine facade despite feeling crushed inside. One thing that kept me going was the thought of my daughters. They were the two amazing miracles that had come out of our marriage. I loved them with all of my heart and wanted to protect them. I did not want our broken marriage to impact what they thought of their father or me. Looking back now, I know I reacted badly. I played the victim: What have I done wrong? This isn't fair! What have I done to deserve this? Why did

The Full Circle

this have to happen to me? Haven't I been through enough? This was a natural reaction for the person I was at that time, as I was operating at effect. This was compounded by the fact that this was my second marriage that had not worked out.

At the same time, it was very different from the break-up of my first marriage. Back then I was relatively young. The decision to leave had been mine. We had reached an impasse on the question of having children. I could not face a future without a family and he did not want a future with children. I felt abandoned and angry that life hadn't turned out the way I expected or planned. I no longer was to have the security of being married and I had lost the sense of family that consisted only of the two of us. My immediate family was not close by and the feelings of loneliness and fear of the unknown crept in.

It was during this time that I met my second husband. Back then the relationship held so much promise. He had also been married before, he said he did not want conflict and he liked the idea of having more children. He had two children already. When I left my first husband, I felt the devastation of it – perhaps because he accepted my decision to leave. I learnt many years later that he was distraught and did not want our marriage to end. Moreover, he knew my happiness involved having a future with children, and he knew he just could not bring himself to concede that point. So, he let me go.

The past is gone and cannot be changed. I do not regret the decision I made back then to change course in my life. Although I had all the sadness and grief associated with the end of this relationship, I was able back then to make that difficult decision and face possible loneliness.

The second time around was different. I had lost that previous strength and felt powerless. I was about to go full circle again with my grief, anger and loneliness, and I was not sure how I would manage.

5: Crushed But Not Broken

> **If you have ever been despondent and completely crushed, emotionally spent and hopeless**
> 1. How did you handle it?
> 2. Are you still there?

_____

_____

_____

_____

_____

_____

Since I have worked through many of my life experiences, I can reflect and know I am not the same person I was back then. I have learnt that though there were times in my life where I felt utterly crushed, I am not broken. I have been able to carry on. I can also recognise that because of the life I was living at the time, I made one bad decision which impacted others. When I decided to start anew with my second husband, it was with a great deal of promise and hope. I left the U.S. and moved to Australia for him. I became the step-mother to his two children, aged eight and ten years, as he had joint custody with his ex-wife. I took care of his children as my own. As I had no family of my own in Australia, I quickly became integrated with his family and friends.

His world became my world. There were many adjustments I had to make. Small simple things like changing the way I cooked and ate – because I had to accommodate him and his family's needs and desires. I was looking after two children without prior experience or knowledge with respect to their care, let alone step-parenting. The climate was different and the people were different from my life in the U.S.

Although, I had lived in Australia for five years as a child, coming back as an adult was a far cry from what I remembered. I was American – something that seemed to be a local source of mockery for my husband and many of the people I encountered. There were many derogatory nicknames for Americans, something I had never experienced before. Many individuals seemed to despise most things American, or maybe it was just a reason to crack a joke at the expense of my heritage. There seemed to be a warped sense of humour which involved having a go at anyone or anything foreign. Perhaps I became the inspiration for their jokes.

As I have lived in Australia now for many years, I have observed that some of these behaviours and attitudes are part of how Australians are. Americans were not the only people who were mocked or made fun of, and it still happens today. The tall poppy syndrome plays into it as well, which I still have trouble understanding. For individuals to be resented, criticised, cut down or attacked because they have been successful at something seems to me an extraordinary way to behave.

Whatever the case, this behaviour towards me was very unpleasant and although I lived with it and attempted to not make it personal, it hurt regardless. As I absorbed all these negatives, it unfortunately meant I became angry and vindictive. There were times in my marriage where I would lash out and insult something my husband loved just to hurt him as I reasoned I had been hurt. My behaviour was ghastly at times and I am not proud of it. I know that I added to the difficulty of our marriage, especially in the way I responded to situations. As you can imagine, most of the time, it just made things worse. I became a shadow of my former confident self, yet, the fear of being on my own again if this marriage failed, made me stay. As bad as it was, I was too afraid to leave him. What would I do? Where would I go?

5: Crushed But Not Broken

I imagined that everything would get better once this or that changed. I became one of those women trapped in a bad relationship who, at the time, felt powerless to do anything about it. So many times people ask: How does it happen? How does a smart, intelligent, strong woman end up being so crushed? Was it the relationship that changed them? All things considered, it is clear, that, at the time, I was living at effect. I absorbed the circumstances and situations around me and just let them play out. I reacted out of hurt and anger. I was not alone, but I was very lonely.

I missed my family and all that was familiar to me – particularly their emotional support. Often times, I could not relate to what was being discussed in conversations. These events would have happened in Australia before I arrived and I was unfamiliar with them, so my sense of feeling obtuse started. I did not think I had much control over what was happening to me, so naturally I thought it was all very unfair. When I felt hurt, my response was to hurt back.

I could say I was just being human. I thought there was no other way. It is a reaction many might have when you feel as though you have no control over your life. This attitude may be similar for those individuals in a relationship with someone who is a substance (alcohol or drug) abuser, someone who has an aggressive personality or someone who cheats on their spouse. The person who is instigating the behaviour is at effect. However, the person who is having the 'injustice' done to them is actually also at effect. This is because you have given your control over to the other person rather than taking control for yourself. If you were taking control and being responsible for yourself, then you would not tolerate any injustice done to you.

When you lose your self-esteem and control over your life, you become lost and disconnected with who you really are. Unfortunately, classes in this sort of thought process are not normally taught. You don't always know for yourself what will bring you happiness and fulfillment. As a result, you learn to behave according to how you feel or have been brought up.

Somehow, as low as I got and as dark as my life seemed, I found the strength to look for ways to get past how I observed myself and my life. This process took a while, and even now I aspire to be the best version of myself possible. I accept responsibility for my past – which is a liberating thought. By doing this, I am able to free myself to move into a brighter future of my own choice. I also know with complete certainty that what I considered to be the worst day of my life was, in fact, the BEST. If things had been different, I may still be living a life which was distressing and filled with feelings of defeat. Now the circle from happiness to despair and back again is complete.

> *"Don't despair over the worst day of your life because it may turn out to be the best!"*
> **– Paulette Archer**

Think about your experiences with setbacks

1. How have they influenced your life?
2. Were these setbacks you had under your control? How did that make you feel?
3. Did you manage to move past or get over the setbacks? How did you do it?

_____

_____

_____

_____

_____

5: Crushed But Not Broken

Health is a Mindset

Because I was somewhat protected in my early childhood I was never made to feel that I was a burden to the family. I had a great deal of support and did not feel alone. This helped me to grow up feeling confident in myself. I have had my fair share of health issues throughout my life and reminiscing, I wondered; "could this all have had to do with my mindset"? As I grew, I regularly suffered from tonsillitis. Eventually, when I was 16, very soon after moving from Australia to Switzerland, it was decided that I needed to have my tonsils removed. It is not much of an operation when you are a small child, but it is a lot more painful and difficult when you are a teenager. After the operation, I was quite ill. I remember feeling alone and scared in the hospital where everything and everyone was foreign to me.

My response had been one of fear and anger. Loneliness and abandonment also raised their head since I had to stay in hospital for a week and did not have the safety of the family around me. Most of the hospital workers spoke French so I could not understand them. Being in hospital in a foreign country was disheartening. Being new in the country meant I had no friends to visit me, which led to my increased loneliness. I longed for my life and friends back in Australia.

Even though I had travelled a great deal growing up, in reality, I found it especially hard to be in foreign surroundings when I was unwell. Just before my sister's wedding, I had to have emergency surgery for a burst appendix. Once again, I was in a strange town where I did not know anyone, and for me at that time, it was traumatic. I was terrified when admitted to hospital initially not knowing what was wrong. Again, I was alone, experiencing anger and fear about my condition and another stay in hospital – another operation without the support of my friends.

Within the first two years of returning to Australia as an adult in my early 30's, I was diagnosed with IBS (Irritable Bowel Syndrome). Eventually, chronic headaches started. Both of these were caused primarily by stress and were thoroughly debilitating. It took quite a bit of time and investigation to ascertain that this resulted from tension. I did not want to believe that my life was so unhappy that it was causing physical symptoms. I was always looking for other reasons than stress for these conditions.

Another fairly major health issue was having a bad skiing injury in which I broke my ACL (anterior cruciate ligament) and had to have a total knee reconstruction. I injured my knee on the first run of the first day of my ski holiday. It was unpleasant to sit in the hotel room in extreme pain when everyone else was out on the slopes. I felt neglected and alone with the thought that my injury was insignificant.

In more recent times, my health issues concern my back. I never dreamed at this stage of my life I would be single and debilitated due to the nerve damage from the bulging disc which has caused permanent damage. The partial foot drop which has occurred causes chronic nerve pain and difficulty with balance and mobility. My back, although repaired, still inflicts pain and imposes certain restrictions. That said, I am able to control how I react to it and have little down time because of it. Presently, I wonder how much of my past health issues could have been changed if my mindset was different?

Louise Hay, in her book *You Can Heal Your Life*, explains how our own beliefs and ideas can cause emotional problems which relate to certain physical maladies. Given this way of thinking, it may be possible that mindset plays a huge role and my most recent health issues (around my back and chronic pain) could be aligned to unresolved issues I may still have. This makes me mindful of my life – where it is and where it is going.

Real Setbacks and Our Responses to Them

In terms of setbacks, these were fairly minor events in my life. The interesting thing is that it was not until I started writing this book and reflecting on my life that I recognised my responses were a result of fear, anger, loneliness and feelings of abandonment.

Teenage tantrums and minor surgeries are one thing; a broken marriage is something else – especially when it is a second marriage that has failed. The anger and fear were multiplied ten-fold and the loneliness sunk in. Once again, the support I thought I needed was no longer there. There was the disbelief of having to go through a divorce – again!

Only this time I was much older and in my mid 50's. There were children to consider, one daughter 14 and the other 20 years old. I did not know what I was going to do. I had left my family and my home country, the U.S., for this man and I didn't want to be wrong again. I did not want another broken marriage. Before the split, I kept hoping things would be better or different somehow. I had pondered that our marriage would eventually be okay when the kids were older, when the business was less stressful or when something else would change.

There were lies and accusations, tit for tat reactions. We fought a lot on just about everything such as his socialising habits and my nagging to name a few. Between the two of us, we had plenty of issues. I can see now that our arguments were about the same "issues" many people have in relationships. But for us, (although we had attended counseling), we couldn't change our behaviour towards each other.

I had lost my trust in him due to being let down on many occasions and the same probably held true for him. I have wondered since then why it went so wrong? When we had issues, it did not help that I retaliated because of what I saw as the injustice of the situation. I may have put up a fighting front with him at times, but inside I was quietly dying. I felt so utterly low. And I was scared. I was scared that he would leave me because I didn't love myself or believe in myself or my ability to function without him.

The Full Circle

In the end, my fears were realised when he did leave me and I was powerless to do anything about it. I was blamed for everything as I had blamed him, and I did not handle the initial loss well. I was exceedingly low at that point in my life and suffered from the horrific tension headaches and IBS. I was physically weak, worn out and emotionally spent.

In our marriage, happiness eluded both of us for ages. For aeons, I wanted to figure out what we could do to be happy. By then, I knew that money, status and possessions were not the answer to happiness. Was it a personality clash which meant that our relationship was always doomed to failure? Was it because we both wanted to be right about how we saw our lives? Was it because neither of us took responsibility for our lives? I know, for me, this was the major reason and my mindset was certainly in victim mode. I was in fact, a perfect victim!

Eventually it no longer mattered what went wrong. For a long time, I continued to be crushed and I did not handle him leaving me with any dignity. That was one of the hardest parts of my journey to recovery. I felt very embarrassed with myself when I thought back about what I did and how I acted. In time, as I worked through it, I took responsibility for my actions and then put them behind me.

Now, I have no problem with it. I did what I did because that was all I knew back then and of course, because I was living at effect. I do not beat myself up over it any more or wallow in regret. It is what it is. In the process of working through everything, I have discovered so much more about myself and about life in general. I reacted to my circumstances out of anger, fear and the perceived idea that I could not do it alone. These things happened to me for a reason. I am who I am now because of it.

Fear, anger and regrets, we all have them

1. Can you recall a time when you responded to a setback either in fear or anger? If you think about that incident now, do you still feel that way? If not, what has changed?

2. If something similar were to happen now, how do you think you would respond to it?

3. Have you ever reacted in ways that you later regretted? Does your behaviour still haunt you? How do you think you could take responsibility for your actions?

4. How will it feel when you have worked through those emotions and put those regrets behind you?

5. Is there anything stopping you from dealing with the issues? Are those really valid reasons or just excuses?

6. What will it take for you to deal with your regrets and move forward?

_____
_____
_____
_____
_____
_____
_____
_____
_____

The Full Circle

If I consider other situations in my life, there were things that were devastating when they occurred, but then they became much less significant later. Believe it or not, now I can even say that about my second marriage. As devastating as it was at the time, it was the best thing that could ever have happened to me. If he had not left me, I might still be with him and seriously unhappy. Even my health improved. As he walked out of my life, so did the tension headaches and IBS! This occurred because these two conditions are highly linked to stress.

I had been on medication for both illnesses. When I first started my self-healing and the self-analysis work with the counselor and in the group sessions, I was asked to be drug free. Any mind-altering substances were not tolerated while doing this work. I managed to eliminate these medications within a month of my separation without any ill effects. My mindset had already changed how I was dealing with my life and, although I did have some stress related to being on my own and living with the uncertainty for my future, my previous symptoms vanished. To this day, I remain drug free and pain free from those ailments.

If I have to think about current setbacks in my life, it has to be my back condition. The difference now is that I no longer live in victim mode. Instead, I do my best under the circumstances. I handle my chronic situation adeptly and I rarely lose a day because of it. I can balance my days well so that I do not overdo it – which could lead to a day of pain. I take time out when needed with no sense of guilt for resting.

I have had a few health issues and some major disappointments throughout my life. Some of my experiences have been quite challenging. Still, there is always someone facing way more than I am. I know what I have done through my personal development to alleviate situations in my life to avoid falling into a dark place like I had in the past. I am grateful for my life and all the lessons which have shaped me into my current version. I know my lessons can be applied to many of you who are facing similar or worse situations in life. Together we can get you back to where you want to be. Finding your feet, claiming your power and regaining your life is achievable, as it was for me.

How Does an 'Anchor' Relate to Me?

Experience bears on how people react to disappointments, in that they may have developed a link or association to an event. This can be as a result of either the intensity or the repetition of the event. When that powerful stimulus is applied to one or more of the five senses (auditory, olfactory, kinesthetic, visual or gustatory), a link is created between your emotional state at that time and your neurology. If the event in question has enough emotional strength, or if it happens often enough, an 'anchor' is created. If your neurology has developed an anchor to a situation or event, then this is how your reaction to it will be every time.

As an illustration of this: If every evening at 7:00 p.m. a husband arrives home drunk and then proceeds to abuse his wife, the wife will most likely develop an anchor to 7:00 p.m. She will more than likely be very fearful and nervous while harbouring hurt and possibly even subdued anger towards him. If one evening he arrives home sober, smiling and is nice to her, it makes no difference. This will be the case since she will still react to him as if he was drunk. Coming in the door, drunk, at the same time often enough has set the anchor. The wife's reaction happens unconsciously. If the emotion is intense enough, it may only take one incident to set an anchor.

Conversely, positive anchors can also be set. If this was a completely different scenario where the marriage was good and the husband cared a great deal for his wife, homecoming each evening may be a cause for great joy. As 7:00 p.m. draws near, the wife may feel a sense of excitement building as she looks forward to a loving embrace and kind words when her husband arrives. If by chance, it happens that one night he comes home drunk and in a bad mood, it will most likely be ignored and treated as just a one-off situation and not a major recurring issue.

> **Consider whether or not you have any emotional anchors/ trigger points in your life**
> 1. Did they result from a setback or traumatic event?
> 2. When did you last experience one of these events? What was your reaction?
> 3. Have you considered that you might need to work through these trigger points so they do not set you off in future? How do you think you can elicit a solution?

_____
_____
_____
_____
_____
_____

People often question why women or men stay in relationships that are abusive. If you are so unhappy, why don't you just leave? There can be many reasons. For some individuals, there is the sense of "if I just try harder, things will get better". You think you are unable to give up on the relationship because it would mean that you are a failure and being a failure would make you feel even more despondent.

Alternatively, the spouse can be an admirable person. The victim then believes that because of this all will be well, and the spouse will no longer be abusive because of the idle promises made after an attack. Or you believe the person who was abusive did not mean it, so another chance will always be given. Perhaps as the victim, you believe you are to blame for the altercation and therefore, deserve what you received. You might promise yourself if *you* try harder *you* will not intimidate the attacker. Fear is also a huge factor which keeps individuals in abusive relationships.

Whatever the case, both parties are victims and have very low self-esteems. Neither has control over the situation. I stayed in my second marriage because I did not want to give up on it. There were good times and I always hoped that everything would change at some stage. I only had control over me – no one else – and I was not functioning at my best in the end. I stayed due to fear of the unknown and also, to save face and prevent another failure. Most importantly, I stayed for my daughters. I did not want the family unit destroyed. I considered myself to be the sort of individual who does not give up easily. I believed that I was in it for the long haul and that was where I had to stay.

Perseverance is a value that sits high on my values list. It seems somehow aligned to success for me. For example, in the past, when working on a difficult assignment, one of the reasons I usually persisted was because I believed it would lead to my happiness. Completing such tasks would mean success and achievement – two of my top values.

If I take this thought to a relationship that I may be in, I would not want to give up on it although I might be struggling, because this would mean I was not successful, that is, a failure. My thoughts would turn to keeping at the task, relationship – whatever it may be – even if I was not getting the desired result. By doing this, I could fool myself into thinking the mere fact that I was still working on the task or "trying" to make things work, translated to happiness and success! At least, I was not giving up yet. And not giving up meant I was not weak, by society's standards. How hypocritical! Have any of you experienced the same kinds of feelings and thoughts?

The Full Circle

This same concept can relate in some way for a person's need to feel like they are in control. In my life, at the time, this was very true. I felt if I was not in control, I lost my power. In those periods of struggle, the control I exercised was not in alignment with taking responsibility. It was because I needed to be right. When I was out of control, I became frustrated, angry and acted inappropriately. In relation to disappointments in my life at that time, there was a sense of regret when things had not gone the way I had anticipated or planned. These emotions of regret and disappointment tended to be intermingled for me, and both occurred then.

If you experience regret, it can be because you consider the decision you had made to be incorrect. You may say to this "I wish I had made a different choice". The disappointment can come about when you wish some event had turned out better. In this case, you might consider, "I wish that event, although beyond my control, had turned out better". If there is constant disappointment in a situation that you feel you have no control over, you can get into the blame mode, become resentful and infuriated – as I did. This is often the case when the disappointment relates to someone close to you – for instance a partner or spouse, parent or child.

The emotional attachment to the disappointment, hurt, and anger intensifies dramatically. In some ways, the greater the expectation, the greater the disappointment can be when an envisioned outcome does not occur. When the reality of the situation sets in, you can become incensed and over wrought. My self-control at the time of my separation was gone for two reasons. First, I *believed* I had no control over what was happening in my life, and I also had no control over the way anyone else may have been operating in the relationship. I did, as I found out later, have the power to do something if I would have taken responsibility for me and my life.

Deep feelings of disappointment can eventually lead to sadness and certainly physical symptoms, as was the case for me. Tonsillitis, burst appendix, chronic tension headaches and IBS would certainly have been caused from my feelings of disappointment and loneliness since our emotions can affect our physical health in so many ways.

Can happiness disappear in the blink of an eye? One minute you are blissfully happy and the next disconsolate? If so, what does this say about happiness and your role or responsibility towards it? This is an interesting question.

It is undeniable that circumstances can occur in your life that are not expected and you can become dispirited about them. Yes, things can change suddenly. In recent history, there have been a number of mass disasters where people have lost their lives, their homes and livelihoods and have had to start all over again with practically nothing. Those conditions, as in this case could be beyond your control. Some people are able to rise above their circumstances and rebuild their lives, while others struggle, never quite managing to get back on their feet.

What is the difference between these two types of people? Are their circumstances really that different? Or is it their response to the situation that makes the difference?

Since I am now in control of my life, the way I respond to situations makes all the difference. I have very few downcast times. When I was not in control, I took on the feelings of everyone else and my happiness was dependent on them. I do not react to situations in the same way anymore, and I feel more at peace in my life. Yet, even as a life coach, I can 'fall off the wagon' and take on the emotions of others and sink into a gloomy state. I am human! The big difference at the present time is that I can snap back much faster. I may have my own personal *pity party*, but then it is over and I move on. I do not let disappointments hold me back or get me down as they previously did.

You Cannot Change Anyone, Only Yourself

Sometimes you may want change from someone you are in a relationship with, but they may not believe that change is needed. Why is it that you think someone else needs to be changed? If you have this belief, two things fall into play. Initially, if you find fault or believe another individual needs to change or do something different, it may actually be what you see in yourself that needs altering. Secondly, you are not taking responsibility for your own life and are blaming the other individual in the relationship. You may be hiding your own insecurities and shifting the blame.

Contemplating my two failed marriages, I resolved what I wanted changed was the attitude of the other person. I wonder now what would have been different if I had been the one with a different attitude. I wanted each person to love me, stand by me and support me, yet believed that it did not happen. Was I perhaps, doing the same thing? Now I no longer worry about the reasons why, and I have stopped trying to figure it out. I do know that divorce was a very big disappointment for me. I regretted, at the time, all that had happened, and was disappointed initially about the outcome. Certainly, now I have changed my thoughts about both situations and know that divorce was the best decision. You can change yourself, not someone else.

If a person says or does something to you that you take to be true, a probable upshot is disempowerment – especially if you allow those people to control you rather than you taking control. Having expectations regarding how events should transpire can also lead to dissatisfaction. This would have happened all through my life.

Frequently, your expectations stem from what had happened in the past when there was a similar occurrence. The end result may have been positive or negative. Nevertheless, your reaction can still be the same as it was the previous time. Your expectations can stem from what you really believe should happen, regardless of whether

5: Crushed But Not Broken

or not you are in much the same situation. Expectations are what we believe the future will hold.

Too many expectations can lead to disappointment because there is always the possibility that someone else will not live up to your requirements. Over the past decade or so, I have had fewer expectations merely due to the fact that my life is so different now. I am less attached to the outcome, which means there is less dissatisfaction for me. Of course, the family dynamic has changed and the types of social activities and functions of earlier days do not exist. Discontent could be evident if I still expected my life to be the same when it is not.

This type of situation can occur for many of you as well. Perhaps through the death of a spouse or divorce, becoming an empty nester or moving to a new location, your situation has changed. If you were to continue to expect the same things now as they had been in the past, it is more than likely you would be disappointed with the outcome.

Occasionally, an old assumption pops its head in, and I become disgruntled. One change that has occurred to me however, is not having as many expectations these days. This was not a conscious decision but occurred because my life is less ordered. I am more spontaneous due to the fact that I am primarily only looking after myself. Spur of the moment decisions are easier now since the children are not dependent on me. I am much more relaxed and often just let things happen. I also have less expectations because my children are grown and living their own lives. My work life is different and, although I interact regularly with people on a daily basis, there are no real expectations around that. I can more easily brush aside negative thoughts if something has not panned out as expected and say "that's the way it was meant to be".

Recently, an example of this occurred. I received a phone call from two friends who were coming to my home for dinner. I was up early preparing the meal and getting things ready. The phone call was to tell me that one of them was ill and could not make it. They were both coming from an hour away, and the other person did not want to travel alone. We made plans to catch up a couple of weeks later. Sure, I was very disappointed because I was looking forward to the catch up with good friends. I had also finished off all the preparations. I could have been upset about the time and effort wasted but, instead, I looked at it in a positive way. My reaction was: "Well, at least now I don't have to cook tomorrow and I can do some work this evening".

Instead of getting upset about all the work and planning I had done, I was understanding and did not need to go into any other emotional state. I know this is just a simple example, but major considerations can be dealt with similarly. I am certain I would not have had the same reaction in my past where I might have been very disappointed, take personal offence or become angry. Once I understood that you can only change yourself and no one else, my life changed.

Thoughts on your expectations

1. How upset do you get about things not working out as planned?
2. How do you react when someone cancels on you?
3. How do you feel when a project you were banking on securing, falls through?
4. How different do you think your reaction would be if you were consciously living at cause?
5. What expectations do you have that perhaps, would lead to much disappointment if they were not met?
6. What can you do about this?

_____
_____
_____
_____
_____
_____
_____
_____

When I think of situations in my first marriage that I could not change, certainly my husband not wanting children was enormous and there was nothing I could do to change him. I did not try to either since he made it quite clear. I did hope with time he would change his mind. When that was not forthcoming, I took steps to change and left the marriage. This had a negative impact on my happiness for quite a while, but I made my decision and was okay with it.

The Worst Thing to Happen Can Be the Best

The realisation that the worst could actually be the best came along fairly soon in my personal development journey. I still felt as if I was in a daze for some time after the separation. I did not quite believe my situation but had to simply accept it. If I am honest here and examine the first marriage as well, I had extreme disappointment when the marriage was over. The grieving process had been going on for a while and, when I finally accepted this fact, I adjusted to it. In my second marriage, I knew for many years that the life I had been leading for so long was indeed, distressing and intolerable. If I was going to continue living the way I was, then it would be way too destructive.

Since I felt incapable of doing something about the situation, having my ex make the decision to leave was the answer I was looking for. I remember my words to my daughter when he left. I said: "I don't know why it is happening. But if we learn and grow from it, it will be worth it". To her, my words may have held a very general meaning relating to why he left us. But in reality, what I meant was that I did not know why he had chosen that moment to pack his bags and leave. What was so different that day from all the days and years beforehand? Why did he wait until I walked through the door to walk out on us?

My words to my daughter were considerably more meaningful than I thought at the time. Possibly I contemplated that it would not really be the end. I thought he might come back and we would work it out. However, as the days turned to weeks, and weeks into months, I knew there was no way I would go back to that relationship. I also knew he would not try to come back. As hard as I thought it was then, I knew the best decision had been made.

There was so much more at stake this time. Even though for a while I lost hope, I regained it as I became stronger, discovered more about myself and who I really was. It was a time of whirlwind emotions. At one point, I started to feel a bit of compassion for him. Later, my feelings changed and I went through more blame, resentment and anger. Perhaps I had not dealt enough with the sadness and grief in the beginning, so it took a while to fully accept without regret, anger, or blame. Mind you most of the emotions I experienced were aimed at me, more than anyone else.

Is Forgiving and Forgetting the Key to Moving Forward?

I have no doubt that what we need to do is forgive, forget and move forward. Although the forget part is at times, harder for me. What about you? I discussed anchors earlier. Since there have been very strong anchors for me with respect to the harder times in my life, it usually demands conscious effort to eliminate them.

I would like to clarify what I mean by the conscious, subconscious and unconscious mind before I go further. This then will give you a better understanding of what I am talking about here. We all have a conscious, subconscious and unconscious mind.

The *conscious* mind is at work when you are aware of what is happening inside and outside of you at that moment. For instance, being aware of how you feel sitting on a chair if it is uncomfortable.

The *subconscious* mind will hold information that can be easily accessed like a memory recall. In this case, let's say you are walking home and at the same time you are talking with someone, perhaps on your phone. When you arrive at your front door you realise you got there without thinking about the way you reached your destination. The information to get home is in your subconscious mind, which is working all the time without you being aware.

Finally, the *unconscious* mind. This area holds all of the information which you have acquired during your life. This is where your values, beliefs and behavioural patterns reside. When a situation occurs which has to do with what is stored in the unconscious mind, this part of your brain will move into your subconscious mind to get the

The Full Circle

information you need at that time. You will become aware of your thoughts, thereby allowing the task to be accomplished.

I have anchors for good and bad events. I know what the anchors are for, and the information of some are stored in my unconscious mind if they have not been used for a long time. If a new situation takes me back to a difficult event in my life; and it is way back in my unconscious mind because I have not dealt with this type of event for a while, the result may not be the best. With the anchor elicited, I may find what comes into my conscious mind is the way I dealt with it before my personal development work, which may not be the best way to deal with it, considering my warped coping mechanisms before my divorce.

Currently, I am able to get rid of any negativity much faster and, in effect, I am reprogramming my unconscious to store this new information for later. If the anchors are elicited often and are positive, then I will be able to eliminate the negativity linked to those past events more quickly. The event comes and goes and is not held onto anymore. The good anchors I endeavour to keep! I mentioned earlier the one relating to the smell of popcorn at the movies. Anchors can be very strong.

If we are going to hold grudges and be angry forever, we will be incapable of true change and happiness. If you do not forgive or forget, you can harbour this discontent in your unconscious and it will affect you in the long run with disappointment, regret and unhappiness since this is the default setting of your mind. Resentment also means you have given your power over to the person who you resent and have lost your control. If you give in to the temptation of holding a grudge, resenting someone, hating or being angry, you are just lowering yourself to their level. Once again, you are causing unhappiness and discontent in *your* life. Of course, this can be damaging if it progresses to health issues or depression.

You may feel justified or even self-righteous in your resentment. This brings me back to the idea that if I respond in this way I would be no better than the person who hurt me, and it does not seem worth it. Today I am able to say to myself it is the other person who has the problem – it is their responsibility, not mine. This does not make me right and them wrong. Instead, what it does say is I take responsibility for me and the way I am and whatever happens for them is their responsibility.

Previously, I did not do this. Rather, there were times I wanted to do something to get back at the so called 'wrongdoer'. On occasion, I was encouraged to get even with the would-be offender. I remember this happening as a child and being told by my mother that revenge is not the best response to situations I may not have been happy with. As an adult, I have seen that many people would gladly retaliate and the scene of clothes being cut up by an unhappy partner or stealing from your boss because you believe he owes it to you for all your hard work, is not uncommon. As a business owner, this has happened. This type of behaviour cannot serve you well in the long run and can lead to regret. Retaliation could lead to further feelings of resentment and anger and create a vicious circle. Grudges and revenge are not a healthy way to behave.

Forgiveness is important. When I was a child, my mother taught me to never go to bed holding a grudge or being angry with someone. She said to forgive and apologise as well, if necessary, so the air is clear. My mother's words have come to me many times in my life, especially when an argument had ensued with my husband before going to bed. Unfortunately, even though I could hear her words, I was at times powerless to act on them.

Other situations which have been relayed to me are the times there may have been an argument between individuals and the person states, "The last words I uttered came with anger – I never had a chance to make things right". This of course happens after the other person in the argument has perhaps died. I have heard of this more than once and believe it could be soul destroying.

I do not remember much about learning how to forget and because of the strong anchors, this could be why it is a little harder for me to do. When I have a clear idea about what happened and why, the forgetting is easier. Very often I am looking for reasons. If the air is cleared between the parties involved, forgetting may be more feasible. I know that clearing the air about a difference of opinion or an argument definitely helps me to forget more easily.

This could be the same for you if you find it hard to forget. Towards the end of the Chapter I will list a few ways that have helped me forgive, forget and move on. Situations have arisen where my clients, friends or even families have had arguments and the reasons are not clear to those looking in on the situation, maybe not even to those directly involved. When I then hear them say, "I will never forgive or forget what so-and-so did to me" it makes me wonder if they can truly find peace in their life, since they never clear the air with each other and stay with the grudge.

This can relate to the depth of the relationship and that arguments are more the exception rather than the norm. To demonstrate what can happen, a situation that was communicated to me about an argument that occurred between a client and her daughter comes to mind.

For a good period of time, my client stayed angry. However, eventually she came around and forgave her daughter. Unfortunately, her husband did not and still holds onto the grudge for the daughter who hurt his wife. This now, at times, causes friction between my client and her husband because he cannot let it go even though it had nothing to do with him in the first instance. I have also been told of grudges held for past issues; where the grudge has continued over a span of decades. Too much energy is wasted on this. Grudges can eat away at the individuals involved.

My grudge-holding and refusal to forgive and forget drained me for ages. In cases where resentment runs deep, it can manifest in physical ailments. The negative emotions can become a toxic influence on a person's body. Understanding myself has made it possible for me to let go and move on.

> **You and your resentments**
> 1. Are you aware of any resentment that you are carrying with you? Why do you feel that resentment?
> 2. Could this be holding you back? In what way?
> 3. How different would you feel if you could put it behind you?
> 4. What do you think it will take to be able to deal with it and move on?

_____
_____
_____
_____
_____
_____
_____

This leads into an interesting question: Who needs to be forgiven most? Is it yourself or those you believe hurt you? Without a doubt, you need to forgive yourself most. I have been taught to forgive through my experiences, personal development and the values instilled while growing up. Influences from church and schooling also had a part to play. Since I have been able to forgive myself, I have been able to forgive others much more easily.

Forgiveness was a huge area in my healing. I believed it was very important for me to heal within myself. I had done many things in my life that I was unhappy about. Because of these past regrets, I felt I needed to give a great deal of forgiveness to myself and others if I was ever going to be truly happy. The many exercises with my NLP helped tremendously.

> *"Be kind to yourself and eventually you too will heal."*
> **– Paulette Archer**

Forgetting may not always mean you have forgiven. However, unless you forgive, you may not be able to forget because it will eat away at you. Perhaps a lack of forgiveness will come back to haunt you. You can forgive and forget, although it may be hard. You can forgive and not forget but forgetting without forgiving may not be possible.

If you find yourself in this situation, here are some ways which you can use to work through the process so you can *forgive, forget and move forward*:

1. Make an attempt to communicate with the so-called offender to patch things up and let them know how you feel about the situation. Remember we are all human and make mistakes. Even in a conflict situation, treat others as you would like them to treat you. In the same way, maybe the shoe could be on the other foot. What if you were the person who needed to say sorry?

2. Keep in mind to forgive as you would want to be forgiven. Remember to first absolve yourself, which may not be easy.

It may be so much easier to excuse others first. Absolution for anything starts with forgiving yourself because it opens the way for exonerating others. It is harder to forgive yourself purely for the reason that you are way harder on yourself than you are on others. If you want to be right with others, you need to be right with yourself first.

3. Talk to someone you can trust or a coach who is not personally attached to the situation.

4. Think about what you could learn from the experience. What has occurred, especially if the hurt came from someone close to you? Is there a possibility for a positive to come out of it?

    For instance, in my past, I have allowed people to hurt my feelings. Perhaps unconsciously for them, but I was easily affected by it. I needed to look at why that may have happened and perhaps look more sensitively to others in the future. I believe that most of the time people are not purposely malicious. Consider why they may have done what they did. Maybe there were extenuating circumstances you did not know about. This morning their best friend may have died, they may have lost their job, had a fight with their spouse. You will not know for certain what is going on for someone else which may affect their behaviour towards others.

    Think of times when *you* may have hurt someone either consciously or unconsciously.

5. Look at the bigger picture. The big picture is about where it is you are heading or what it is you had aimed for in the first place. What outcome were you looking for?

    Often times, you can look at all of the little steps in a situation. You get caught up in every little detail. If forgiveness is the outcome, perhaps you need to pay more attention to what the overall situation is about and then you may find it is not as bad as you thought. The situation has already occurred, so you cannot change it. All you can change is your mindset around it. I have been known to make a mountain out of a molehill. Perhaps you have, too? When this happens, it helps me to look at the bigger picture. If I think this is serious I ask, "Compared to what"? This helps to put things in perspective. There can always be something way worse than what you are experiencing.

6. How are you reacting to the situation? Even if you cannot control certain circumstances, you can control your reaction to them. So, look at why you are feeling the way you are and be accountable for how you would prefer to feel about it. Look at your negative self-talk and get rid of it – turn those negatives into positive affirmations as we did in Chapter 1. (Steps to Writing an Affirmation page 263)

7. If you observe that resentment or conflict is causing a lot of stress, use steps to clear your mind, such as getting into a state of relaxation and/or meditation. Sometimes taking a break from worrying about something can bring fresh perspective and energy. Do give yourself time – there is no rush.

8. Writing a letter (which you never send) can also be instrumental in helping with the forgiving and forgetting process. You can write this letter to yourself for self-forgiveness as well as writing to anyone else you feel the need to make amends.

"Remember, if you take responsibility for your life and actions, then you will be able to throw away the victim mode and change your negative words to positive and empowering ones."
– Paulette Archer

There has been a lot to understand and take in with this chapter. If you are feeling like you have hit rock bottom you may feel crushed. There are so many things you can do to remedy this. But I wonder – you most probably have a fair amount of self-doubt at the moment if you are feeling this way, so steps to rid that would most assuredly be needed to move past it. I know self-doubt has surfaced on more than one occasion in my life, which we will see right now.

6: Self-Doubt – Fear of the Unknown

"If we fear the unknown, then surely we fear ourselves."
– Bryant H. McGill

Even now, occasionally self-doubt creeps in for minute reasons. Perhaps a project I am working on is not going correctly, or I am struggling to figure things out. Sometimes I get frustrated because I am having difficulty with a certain concept. Doubts start to surface. I think "Will I ever figure this out" or "Why is this so hard for me"? In these instances, I quickly fall back into old habits and tell myself that what I am trying to do is way beyond me. All my positivity peters out immediately.

The problem is not that I cannot do something, but, I hear the voices which have told me in the past that I am not smart enough. There were times when I was being told I wasn't smart enough by other people. It started to form a part of my belief system. This is where those voices- the voices of self-doubt- originated. At one time in my life (while I was still married), I believed what the voices were saying was true. Then, listening to the self-doubt took me to a low dark place where I did not feel as though I was worth much.

Fortunately, I never let that dark place win. Instead, I started to discover many positive things about myself. Somehow, I held one thread of hope, which kept me hanging on until I could climb out of that hole. The good thing now is even though self-doubt occasionally rears its ugly head, I can tell it to "get lost" and I can do for myself what my self-doubt was telling me I could not. In a sense, writing this book has been a reminder of how far I have come and has assisted tremendously in my healing.

> **Recount when you last doubted yourself**
> 1. What was it all about?
> 2. Was it the truth?

_____

_____

_____

When I understood what others said or thought about me made no difference, I reached a turning point. I could appreciate it is how *I* feel about myself that matters, not other people's opinion. In my past, it was not always easy to have this mindset when I had a strong negative view of my life to begin with. I now know unequivocally the reasons I formed those negative ideas was because a large part of what I was looking at was how others judged me. I allowed that to control my thoughts. This is why self-love is so important. Once I began to love myself completely, it no longer made any difference what others thought or felt about me.

This is one of the key questions that self-doubt raises for me. Do other people's opinions matter? We are all unique individuals; no two of us are the same. My accomplishments are different from those of my peers or acquaintances. Do I need to compare myself to them, or am I okay with my skill set?

No, I do not need to compare and I am okay with my skill set. It is interesting to know that so many people seek the approval of others. They are constantly looking for approval from the outside. When that does not happen, self-doubt can surely surface and it can do so instantly. I have experienced feelings of confidence one minute and doubt my abilities the next. Has the same thing happened for you? Did those thoughts of self-doubt surface because of what others had thought or said about you?

As a child and young adult, my parents positively reinforced me by telling me I was doing a great job or encouraging my efforts at accomplishing a task. They might have told me I was intelligent or a hard worker. At those times there was no reason for self-doubt. I did not have a competitive nature, so I wasn't ever trying to do better than anyone else. I was only trying to do the best for me.

Once I finished my University studies and began my working career, the same support I had previously was no longer there. It was at this time that self-doubt started to surface. If I did find difficulties, I had only myself telling me I was doing a great job and sometimes I believed that not to be the case. I may have also been told by a teacher or other individual that I could do better. If I thought I had done the best job I could do and was told I could do better, it was easy for me to doubt my abilities.

When I was married, those same doubts surfaced once again. It was easy then to change quickly from a positive to a negative mindset. What made that rapid change? What happened to set the self-doubt in, where had the belief in myself gone? Since I had lost my support, what I knew about myself at that time was not enough. I believed what everyone told me about me and never considered the falsehood of their claims.

Nowadays, as I continue my journey of self-development, I am well aware that consistently engaging in activities that keep me uplifted and positive are very important. Mixing with positive and happy people, keeping my gratitude journal up to date, meditating, reading positive and motivational literature, having regular exercise and keeping fit and healthy all add to keeping any self-doubt from creeping in.

The Full Circle

Self-doubt is a natural human reaction. What is important is not to let it control your life. This journey was difficult because in addition to other possible influencers of my self-doubt, I had the voices telling me for a long time that I was not smart enough or good enough. You too may have these voices and unlike me you may not have had the positive reinforcement I had as a child. But I took action to change what I did not like about my life. You can too.

I will be discussing a little later some tools that you can employ to overcome self-doubt. These tools have now been instrumental in helping me and keeping the self-doubt away. However, self-doubt often comes about when you compare yourself to others. Keep in mind that you are on a completely different journey from me and everyone else on this planet. No longer pay attention to what anyone says or thinks about you. Get rid of the negative influences in your life. Stop the negative self-talk, and if you think you have been a failure at something, regard it as a learning experience and then turn it into a positive.

I often have clients who say how unhappy they are in a situation, adding how it is beyond their control. It is my job to help them understand that this is not the case. They can take action to make the changes they want in their lives. I simply assist them to find ways in which they can do this. A big part of this is that they develop self-love, learn to believe in themselves, understand the concept of living at cause or at effect; and making changes in their life so that they take responsibility for creating what they desire.

"When you doubt your power, you give power to your doubt."
– Honore de Balzac

> **Contemplate the following questions**
> 1. Are you faced with any situations right now that you are not happy about but don't think you can change? What are they and why don't you think you can change them?
> 2. If you could, how would you go about it and why?
> 3. How would you feel if you could change these situations?
> 4. How much better could your life be with this change?

_____
_____
_____
_____
_____
_____

What Drives You to Doubt Yourself?

There are many external catalysts of self-doubt. They can include mixing with people who are in victim mode or who try to steer you from your course. These are people who want you to agree with them in their negativity. If you are in an environment in which you are not comfortable or doing something that you do not want to do, you are not taking responsibility for your life. Another catalyst could be working on a project and hitting a stumbling block you find difficult to remedy. This was often the reason my self-doubt reappeared. Examples of causes for self-doubt could be failing at accomplishing a goal, failing in a relationship, or losing a job. These were some of mine. What could yours be?

The Full Circle

> **Look at some catalysts of self-doubt**
> 1. In what area of your life are you least confident?
> 2. What abilities do you doubt the most and why?
> 3. Are there certain situations where you doubt yourself more? Why is this?
> 4. When do you feel the most confident? Why do you think this is?
> 5. Do you believe change is impossible for you?

_____
_____
_____
_____
_____
_____

I call to mind quite vividly my self-doubt returning when I was hired for a nursing job, which initially had played quite a big role in helping me to rebuild my life and become independent again. In fact, it was a surprise to get the job in the first place. During my second marriage, I had not worked a great deal in the nursing sector. Working full time was something I did when needed in our family business. This alternated with times when I worked quite long stretches helping out in various roles. I had various nursing jobs over those years, which I thoroughly enjoyed, but because of the family business, I did not have long term employment in nursing.

After my separation, I was not sure what kind of work I would be able to do. So much had changed since I was last in the job market. I studied to become a Life Coach and enrolled for a computer course to help me in my coaching business. One of the assignments of the course was to apply for jobs. I found jobs in the nursing sector and applied for them, even though I did not have half the qualifications. I doubted I would ever get what I considered to be a decent nursing job, so I was not surprised when at first, I received no feedback from many I applied to. Mind you, I was only looking to fulfill a course requirement, not that I actually wanted a job. After all - I had my coaching business. What was essential was completing the computer course assignments.

Six months after completion I was contacted by one of the clinics I had applied to. It turned out they had hired someone else but she did not work out. They had kept my CV because I was also qualified as a life coach and, in the end, I got the job. It seemed all my self-doubt had been unfounded. I was overjoyed with this opportunity. I was still coaching; however, I took the job because it gave me the chance to work with more people on a daily basis. The position was challenging as I had not worked in that area of nursing previously. There was so much to learn. The self-doubt set in again. "Would I ever be able to learn what I needed in order to do a satisfactory job?"

I took some time off, several months after I started, for a trip that was organised prior to my employment. It came at a good time because my head had been spinning with all of the new information. My trip was excellent, but I was nervous about returning to the job because, once again, the self-doubt resurfaced. I believed I would not remember a thing upon my return. This caused me a great deal of anxiety. To my surprise, I found I remembered things I didn't remember learning in the first place and, after that, I went from strength to strength in that position.

Years later, when I wanted to leave this job, my self-doubt took over once again. Would I be able to get another job? And if I decided to go back to full time coaching, would I be able to earn enough money to keep going?

The Full Circle

After debating the next line of action for quite some time, I became aware that I had not been immersing myself in my own self-development. I had fallen off the wagon, so to speak. It was clear that this part of my life was lacking. I started getting back into my motivational reading. I attended some courses and workshops. I started volunteering again, which I had missed doing for a couple of years. It was amazing! I also learnt to love myself again.

As I did all of this, the voices of self-doubt disappeared. At that point, I made a decision – yes, I could do it. I could start out on my own. I was ready for a change. I was restless and believed my life was way too important to be living and working in an environment that I was no longer enjoying, just to have a job. After all, as a coach, I had helped others make these decisions, so I certainly could make them for myself. I could do what was needed to go out on my own. I started believing in myself and my abilities once again and the self-doubt vanished.

The day I made the decision to resign, I had nothing concrete set in place. Yet, I felt totally liberated having made the decision to leave my job. After I made the decision, my whole attitude and behaviour changed. I knew within myself that everything would fall into place. I had the time and space to map out my plan. To set up my business, I took what I knew beforehand to add to my new journey. Not long afterwards, I started working in the area of personal/leadership development in my own coaching business.

Believing that I might not find work or a path in my life that I would be happy in when I was considering leaving my job, was a self-limiting belief. This experience taught me once again, how much limiting beliefs can be a driver of self-doubt. Being out of integrity and/or doing something that does not align with your own values, being worried about what others think, losing your self-love, or just having a negative attitude about yourself and a low self-esteem can also be catalysts for self-doubt.

Who Says You Aren't Good Enough?

As an adult, you may not feel like you are good enough because growing up, you might not have received much support or encouragement from your parents, teachers or significant others. Growing up, I always felt that I could do whatever I set my mind to. My parents always encouraged me to try new things and expand my knowledge. I graduated from high school feeling confident and carried that with me into my university days. So, what changed to make me lose my confidence? At what point did self-doubt start to creep into my life? I became aware of it after leaving home and not having my normal support system – my parents – near me.

As I started working through my personal development, I could see that around my 30's to 40's, I started listening to other people's opinions that I was not good enough. When I heard similar comments more than once, I started to believe it. I would compare my life to others and perceive that I came up short. I would think "they must be right, I'm not good enough". This self-realisation demonstrated to me how easy it is to come to these false conclusions based mostly on what others think and do.

We are all individuals. Like snowflakes, no two people are exactly the same. We live and breathe the same air, but all the rest is dependent on you alone. Your values, your perception of the world, how you react to your environment – are all about taking charge of your life. I started to see that nothing in my life is more important than living a great life on my terms and loving myself at the same time. I believe that, once this is the case, everything falls beautifully into place. When I have positive thoughts about myself and my life, the "stars shine"!

> *"All that we are is the result of what we have thought. The mind is everything.*
> *What we think we become."*
>
> **– Buddha**

Want to Overcome Self-Doubt? Try Out These Tools.

Several negative emotions associated with self-doubt are frustration, anxiety, fear, anger or depression. If you let these emotions overtake you, they can lead to physical maladies as well.

The question is: If you recognise any of these symptoms in your life, how can you then overcome them?

Start by:

1. Identifying self-doubt and accepting that it is present in your life.
2. Being willing to overcome it.
3. Thinking about times in your life that self-doubt surfaces.
4. Thinking of the stimuli that triggers these feelings. Is there a regular pattern there? Is there a certain memory that initiates it? Like the way a partner, boss or other individual may have treated you? Consider the negative anchors.
5. Thinking of times when you may have felt this way, but then had a positive outcome to something that you feared.
6. Understanding that self-doubt is normal and many people suffer from it at different times in their lives.

Writing a positive affirmation

(Follow the Steps to Writing an Affirmation in the Resources page 263, then look at the following.)

1. Is there one area of your life where your self-doubt is high? Write down what it is. Now rewrite that phrase in the positive, as if doubt was not a factor anymore, and you had complete confidence in your ability. This becomes your affirmation.

   (As an example, change "I am such a loser and will never be good enough to attract the right people into my life", to "I love myself and all the experiences which have moulded me into the wonderful being I am today and I attract the most amazing people into my life".)

2. When you read the affirmation out loud, how does it feel to be speaking those positive words?

3. Does it feel comfortable to say these words? If it does, great! If not, consider for a moment why that would be. (If you are still having difficulty with this, I might suggest that you revisit Chapter 1 on self-love.)

4. Start to use the positive affirmation and forget what you told yourself beforehand.

5. Are there other areas in your life where you could be more positive? If so, repeat the exercise for each of those areas until you have a list of affirmations.

_____
_____
_____
_____
_____

How Can You Take Conscious Steps to Change?

1. Ask yourself these questions: What do I doubt? Is it the ability to change jobs, or go back to school and learn a new skill? Is it something that I have always wanted to do, that I am passionate about? Does it involve leaving a bad relationship and going out on my own?

2. Look at why you doubt your ability to take control. What is holding you back from doing what you want? What makes you feel paralysed to even attempt it? Is it fear or just simply that you are not sure you can do it? Stop the negative talk in your head.

   An exercise you can do goes as follows:

   - Take out your journal and write down your negative thoughts.
   - Now read them through.
   - Change these negative thoughts to positives.
   - Now read the positive thoughts out loud as affirmations.
   - Make a conscious effort to think those positive thoughts on a regular basis.

These affirmations could be such things as: "I am knowledgeable and excel in my work", "I find exercise and keeping fit easy and enjoyable", "I am a fabulous cook and adore making healthy, delicious meals every day". "I find working in my garden therapeutic and relaxing and my plants looks awesome!" "I am grateful for all relationships in my life and give and receive love willingly and completely."

These are some of my affirmations and examples of ways to engage in positive self-talk. It is about focusing on what you can do rather than what you can't. If you think you can't, then you won't. If you expect a negative outcome, that is exactly what will happen.

3. To banish the self-doubt, you need to work at having faith in yourself and your abilities. Perhaps in your childhood, or even as an adult, you were told that it was impossible to do something, or you weren't smart enough. This does not mean you cannot do something now. Set some goals around what you want and be very clear about them.

4. Journaling is a great tool to use. I like to journal. Writing down my thoughts about how I am feeling is marvelous therapy. Once you have recognised and written down how you feel, you can add steps to remedy this.

5. Letter writing is similar to journaling; however, this is where you 'write a letter' to people who have been a negative influence in your life. (This is similar to what we spoke about in the forgiveness process, page 128-130.) When I write this letter, I explain everything about my feelings regarding the situation. This assists me in dealing with the doubts. Sometimes the letter is written to me. (You might not want to write this letter in your journal because it never gets sent, and more times than not, it is destroyed which completes the process.) The objective is to download those emotions and learn to express them in a healthy way.

6. Whatever you do, think in terms of taking small steps. Today you might start looking for that new job or start writing 500 words if book writing is your goal. Tomorrow it could be sending out resumes or writing 1000 words for that book. These are examples of steps I took in my own life. If I had not taken those steps, I would not be working in the great environment I am now, nor would I be writing this book! Perhaps you need to hone in on your skills to get a new job. Perhaps you would like to take up a hobby to stretch yourself.

The Full Circle

I recall a time in my life when I was at a seminar where we had to do something to get out of our comfort zone. An artist came to talk and show us how to do a life drawing. We had a live model whom we had to draw. Of course, I completely doubted my ability to do anything more than a scribble. The only way I could draw people was to make 'stick men'!

I was planning to sit this exercise out. I had told myself "I don't need this, I have no interest in art – who cares if I know how to draw, I don't". But then I decided to face my fears, take things seriously and do it anyway. I was avoiding the exercise because I was afraid of being made fun of by anyone who would see my drawing – which I was convinced would be dreadful. My other fear was failing at the task. If it was not attempted, I could not fail – that made sense, I considered. By the way, this was the very reason this exercise was given to us!

I bit the bullet and concentrated carefully during the lesson and, to my amazement, I actually had a pretty respectable drawing in the end. Now, this was quite a life changing experience for me. It proved to me that maybe there are many times in my life I have self-doubt, and yet, find it is totally unfounded. Similarly, as with scuba diving, how would I know if I liked something or not if I never tried it?

7. Another step to take is to focus on the exceptional moments in your life and celebrate your wins.

8. Surround yourself with positive people and read positive motivating literature. This really helps me. Often a book or article about someone who has achieved greatness despite huge obstacles brings me around. It makes me think: if they can do it, so can I!

9. Have a look at what you want and how to obtain it. And certainly, know that nothing will change if you do not take action.

6: Self-Doubt – Fear of the Unknown

10. Live life within your set of values and do not buy into what others think you should do – live your life for you. Do you know what your values are? If not, remember we will be taking a good look at values in Chapter 8.

11. And finally, DO NOT HOLD ONTO THE PAST!

"When self-doubt is overcome, you are able to get on with your life and accomplish the goals you have set out to achieve. You can move forward, change course if need be, and make any necessary changes to your life based on your values system. When you are living within that frame of reference, you are in integrity and feel great about yourself. You will have a renewed sense of self and more confidence to take on the world."
– Paulette Archer

Everything you have undertaken so far has demonstrated you are learning the steps you need to take to grow into the best person you can be for yourself and those around you. If you can already feel some change in your thinking and you like how you feel, then continue reading. If you want to continue to grow, you will want to continue to learn more about yourself and the world around you.

Congratulations on coming this far with me in this full circle journey. The idea is to get rid of these negative circles of your life that keep you stuck, which has been apparent in the discussion so far. Now let's get some positive circles rolling!

7: Learning and Growing

"I am always ready to learn, although I don't always like being taught."
– Winston Churchill

In my early childhood, I experienced what was then the typical suburban American lifestyle. We were a family of four. Dad worked, Mum stayed home and we spent our free time visiting friends, having block parties and getting involved with school and church activities. In my mind it was a fairly normal existence. I knew nothing else at that time. We did what our friends did, which was pretty routine back then. The people we knew and lived around were all born and raised in the U.S. My parents were second or third generation American and our community was much the same.

It was only when we moved to other countries around the world that I understood clearly that our normal before I was nine years old was sometimes quite different to the normal in other places where I lived. When we moved, I started to learn about different people, places and cultures. In a way, it opened my eyes to how much more there was to experience in this world than the one state in the U.S. I had come from.

Today, with global travel and immigration, societies are much more of a cultural melting pot. If you do not travel, you can still learn so much about different cultures from your neighbours, workmates, friends and even movies, cultural events, television and so on. Now, when I think of my average neighbourhood restaurants, I can eat French, Thai, Greek, Indian, Chinese, German - the variety is endless. In my early life, it was American alone. Presently, I can shop for anything I want either from a physical store or online. These days you do not necessarily need to travel the world to experience different cultures.

> **Describe your normal life**
>
> What is normal for you?

_____

_____

_____

_____

_____

Even now that I am much older, I acknowledge what I considered a normal childhood growing up is quite different from what children experience today. Family structures have changed. Today, it is quite rare for one parent to stay at home and look after the children as most families need two incomes to keep up with the cost of living. Even some occupations and leisure activities have changed significantly since I was at school. My norms are different from those of my daughters. Each generation adapts to new societal benchmarks.

You learn from your parents, and also from your peers and people around you. Most families consisted of two parents when I was growing up, and divorce or marriages between different cultures or ethnicities were uncommon. Yet, today, mixed marriages are widely approved of in most countries. It is no longer taboo to get divorced, in many cultures. Sadly, statistics also show that almost half of marriages end in divorce. In fact, in most Western cultures, it is quite acceptable. And for many, living together in a de facto relationship is commonplace. The incidence of single women or men having children due to the advances in IVF technologies, as well as same sex couples having children, all have an impact on the family dynamic.

What this illustrates is that your notion of normal is constantly shifting. Change is inevitable and unavoidable. Learning and growth, on the other hand, is optional. The world may change around you but if you chose to ignore it, it is unlikely that you will acquire the information to expand your knowledge. Sometimes changes in a person's life can usher in a mind shift. A mind shift is a change in your perception and your focus on life. Because your situation or circumstances change, you can start to view the world through fresh eyes. This can be either a positive or negative.

After my second divorce, the life I had known for many years came to an end. Everything I had been used to, changed dramatically. Now I was on my own and not in a very good head space. My fears and insecurities assailed me. Some might say that my feelings were quite normal and that is very true. But if I had stayed in that negative place, who knows where I would be now? I decided I wanted a change and it took this mind shift, regarding how my life was versus how it could be, to happen before I started to really transform on the inside.

The Full Circle

> **Think about learning and growing**
> 1. Is it something that excites you or terrifies you?
> 2. Why do you think this is?
> 3. Have you ever experienced a mind shift where new knowledge has completely changed the way you approach, think about or do things?
> 4. What was that experience like?

_____

_____

_____

_____

_____

A mind shift has to do with someone changing course from where they are, or have been, to where they want to go. After my separation, I knew that I did not want to stay depressed. I wanted to start to feel good about my life. In the process of personal development, I have had plenty of mind shifts. What is so powerful about a mind shift is it often involves moving away from something that has been ingrained in your life. The change is often difficult, but it is so worthwhile. Mind shifts challenge your beliefs and thinking. They become a new reality about your life and your relationships. Through learning, you decide to head in a different direction than where you were heading before.

When you grow emotionally, your previous thoughts and feelings change in a very positive way. This change frees you from the path you were on and opens new possibilities. When you open your mind to other concepts, you become a different person, so to speak, with a fresh way of thinking and a spring in your step. Once you become aware that there can be something different in your life and you are receptive to it, this is when the shift can occur. Sometimes it is referred to as the 'light bulb' or 'ah-ha' moment.

> **If you've had an 'ah-ha' moment recently**
> 1. What did it change in your life?
> 2. Is there anything you are aware of in your life that needs to change, or you need to evolve, but you have not put into action?
> 3. What will it take to get you to act on it?

_____

_____

_____

_____

Have you ever heard the saying "When the student is ready, the teacher will appear"? In your life, you may often hear things you do not take in, for whatever reason. Your mind filters out the information because it is not something it can relate to at the time. In addition, there may be too much going on in your life for you to absorb this information, or you do not think it is relevant. You might be aware that change is needed, but somehow, you find yourself resisting it.

You may want to leave a job but stay, as you may be in the middle of a project and you are waiting for the right time (which may never come). Or you want to end a relationship and, once again,

The Full Circle

the time does not seem just right. Then one day, there is an ah-ha moment – when you hear something that makes you stop and take notice. It could be what you have heard before, yet, at the time took no notice or action. Too often, that light bulb moment comes as a result of a tragedy – a death, an illness, a divorce, a job loss.

I have had many ah-ha moments, and big ah-ha moments came when I was faced with divorce. When I had gone through numerous surgeries on my back, the light bulb went on. I finally acceded, that to keep me at my best, there were certain things I needed to do or not do, and I could not ignore them any longer. Because of my fear of change, I did not take action until I was forced to by those circumstances.

It is far better to be proactive, than wait until it is too late or until situations are forced upon you to make change. If you are ready for a mind shift, then you become more open to change and many opportunities present themselves to you. Can you consider where you could start shifting your mind from where it is now to a much better place? I venture a guess that you are reading this book because there is something that is not working in your life right now. Together we can make change happen. Altering your mindset about what is possible is a great way to start.

Be grateful for what you have – start a gratitude journal. Quit talking about 'ifs'. Write down a list of things that fall into this category and look at ways of modifying your behaviour. Be 'selfish' by looking after yourself. Itemize your needs and make sure you are taking care of them. Look at your values and see if you are living within your values set. How are your relationships going? Are you happy with your financial and work situation? Do you believe that you deserve more? Be proactive. Be accountable for your transformation and quit thinking or talking about it. Take Action Now!

7: Learning and Growing

"Trust yourself – get away from your self-doubt. Take action to do it now."

– Paulette Archer

Change – there's that word again

1. Have you ever been forced by circumstances to make a change? How did it feel?

2. If you were aware of the situation and that change may be needed, why did you wait until there was no choice?

3. Do you see things might have been different if you had been proactive rather than being forced to react?

4. Do you suspect this will alter how you view change, growth and learning in the future? If so, how?

5. If you were to start a gratitude journal today, what would your first three entries be?

6. What steps do you suppose you can make right now to grow, learn and prepare yourself for the road ahead?

_____
_____
_____
_____
_____
_____

Does Learning Only Happen When We Open Our Minds to It?

The best learning happens when you open your mind to it. However, acquiring knowledge can occur just by being exposed to ideas or concepts which you encounter daily in your life. Being aware of what is happening around you can potentially point you toward gaining new skills and making change. You may hear or read something when you least expect and this could trigger a desire for change. It occurs because, prior to this moment, you may never have been exposed to or thought of it.

As a means of explanation, many years ago a friend wanted me to take meditation classes. Meditation was not anything that I had considered practicing, but I went along to have a look and to support my friend. I could not imagine at the time that it would be beneficial to me, so I did not continue with the lessons. It was not until the past decade that I revisited meditation – once again, not because I wanted to but as a result of attending a seminar wherein our class was put through the steps. It was only then that I finally saw what was available to me if I was willing to commit to the practice. I had heard it all before, yet it was only at this time, 40 years later, that the light bulb went on for me with regards to daily meditation.

This example demonstrates that when I was not open to learning something, it did not happen. Whereas, years later the same suggestion was acted upon because I was then ready for the information. It goes back to the old saying "when the student is ready, the teacher will appear".

Physically Growing is Easy, but What About Your Mental State?

Growth occurs through education and learning which you can make a conscious decision to do, or purely through interaction

7: Learning and Growing

with the world around you. As you get older, you develop new life skills by following your parents, peers and role models. These skills can in turn, take you on new and interesting journeys. Growth begins from birth, and much of what your knowledge consists of is picked up through examples and from those with whom you have the most contact. When a baby starts to walk, what would happen if the first time he fell, he just said; "That's it, I'm not doing this"? The world would be full of people scooting around on their bottoms! So, the baby falls many times until he walks. He grows with each new step. Physically his size changes, so does his emotional growth.

Contact with others gives you basic socialisation skills. When you start school, you learn all about reading, writing and math, etc., as well as about interpersonal communication through your interactions with others. Once again, if a child made a mistake while learning to talk and just gave up, she would not be able to verbally communicate with others. As you go through school, in the older grades, you gain more specific knowledge so that you can function satisfactorily in life and society. But learning in school is just the beginning. Once all of your formal education is over, you acquire some of life's lessons as you have new experiences within the world around you.

For instance, rarely do you take marriage lessons or parenting lessons before you embark on those milestones in your life. Nevertheless, you get married and have children and learn as you go. Throughout life, many of you go on to gain even greater skills in the way of conventional education or through specific courses for any area of life in which you want to improve or gain knowledge. You have the potential to grow daily if you choose.

All of this schooling can lead to further enrichment and ultimately, success for each of you. This can vary from person to person. This mindset of learning, growing and changing is even more important now than it was 20 years ago. The world is changing very rapidly.

If you want to get ahead, you need to embrace this and diversify. I have always done some sort of further education in my life, whether it was for my emotional wellbeing, my intellectual improvement or just to learn something new. If I want to keep up with the world and be on top of my game of life, and also to be useful to future generations, I will continue to expand my knowledge base. Growth through training and study can lead to a more complete and interesting life. Your curiosity can lead to discovering new ways of doing almost anything you choose. You can grow spiritually as well, which has the potential of you gaining more satisfaction in life.

There is a strong movement now toward personal development for individuals alone as well as for business leaders. This can result in better management of teams in the workplace and ultimately, more job satisfaction. Through personal development, you can identify what your values are and if you are living within your values set. This is the case regardless of whether you are an individual employee or a leader of an organisation. Most businesses have mission statements and these may or may not fall into alignment with your own values. If you are working in a job just for the money, but do not agree with any of their policies and procedures, it stands to reason that your job satisfaction could be low.

Furthermore, if the head of your company is only interested in money and hates what he is doing, it is more likely that job satisfaction for all workers will be low. With personal development, each and every individual is able to identify where it is in their life they are feeling unfulfilled and perhaps unhappy. Skills can be developed to enhance communication within the organisation. With good communication, the staff and leaders can verbalise

7: Learning and Growing

their dissension or unhappiness and appropriate steps can be taken to remedy the situation. Also, if all employees are given the opportunity to share their ideas and thoughts with management, it shows that the company values the part each and every staff member plays.

With personal development, you learn to understand yourself, which in turn assists you in understanding others better. When a leader of an organisation works closely with the employees and works toward the general good of the entire group, rather than meeting only their own personal needs, there is bound to be more harmony.

Acquired knowledge and growth is what affords access to the many inventions and developments that we now enjoy in our lives. Growth can contribute to an individual being able to overcome a disability. It can result in higher earning potential and a better status for all. You can do more with new information and expanding your intelligence.

There are opportunities everywhere to improve your skill set or to obtain new ones to help you develop personally and professionally. If you take the initiative to learn something because you choose to, rather than because you have to, this will impact your life more. If you are not motivated through formal study, there are still many ways for you to become educated. You can gain information by following what others are doing and by being guided by these teachers and mentors.

Typically, the higher the interest in growing, the greater the growth. Opportunities surround you daily. Without even trying, you can learn from the TV and radio. You can gain knowledge from reading books, newspapers or magazines; and also, by attending established courses at schools, universities, technical colleges, over the internet or home studies, to name a few. With the internet, your further education is just a keystroke or mouse click away. Just about anyone will tell you where to find answers – Google it!

> *"There is no excuse these days for you to say you have no opportunity to learn and grow."*
> **— Paulette Archer**

There is so much knowledge available and so many great opportunities for us all. As evidence of this, there are incredibly inspiring stories of young people being extraordinarily inventive simply because a topic grabbed their interest and they took the time to research it or learn to do something for the benefit of many.

In one case, 14-year-old Jack Andraka invented a new, inexpensive and fairly accurate way to test for pancreatic cancer. Or consider 10-year-old Kathryn Gregory who invented 'Wristies' which are fuzzy sleeves worn beneath coats and mittens to keep your wrists warm, just because her wrists always got cold in the winter. As an adult she is now the CEO of Wristies, Inc.

In third world countries where it seems impossible for some to get ahead, others thrive and make life better for themselves, their family and their community. In Afghanistan Kamila Sidiqi at age 19 was left alone to care for her siblings with no means to provide for them. Despite the brutal regime in Kabul she became a successful entrepreneur and role model. She made a difference to improve conditions for her family and community by learning to sew and make clothing which she sold to shops. Eventually, she had enough orders to employ other girls and women and developed training classes. Now she runs her own consultancy firm aimed at helping women start their own enterprise.

Throughout the ages, there are many examples of life changes because someone has taken the opportunity to learn and grow.

7: Learning and Growing

> **The ability to learn is available to everyone**
>
> 1. If you had an opportunity right now to sign up for a course where cost and time was not an issue, what course would you choose?
> 2. What have you found is the easiest way for you to learn? Is it through reading, listening, practicing or interacting?
> 3. In what area of your life would you like to learn and grow?
> 4. In what area of your life do you most enjoy learning?

_____

_____

_____

_____

_____

_____

Growing impacts your life by taking you to a higher standard. If you are open to new experiences, you will change and so will everything else in your environment.

Bear in mind however, that change can lead to perceived negative results. For example, when two people are in a relationship and one grows and the other does not, it can lead to conflict. In the same vein, you may change your circle of contacts because you find through your growth and development, you change. Those people with whom you previously interacted may not gel with you in the same way, which may mean some relationships will change. There is a saying that; "friends are there for a reason, a season or a lifetime". Your growth is a big catalyst for this. Some relationships adapt and change as you do, others will wane. But as you learn, grow and change, there is also the opportunity to meet many new people who can impact your life in a positive new way.

Can I Stop Learning Now?

Even though this book is titled *The Full Circle*, I have discovered my life certainly has seen many circles of development and prosperity. The many circles in life teach me that the potential is there to never really stop growth. Just like a circle, no matter where you start, there is no end. There is always something more life can offer. There is always a potential for improvement if you are willing. Because of your unique life experiences, you develop differently from everyone else. Some people may choose to learn from their experiences, grow and move forward. Others may not be ready for change and for them, their life experiences can be different.

Life offers ceaseless educational opportunities. You can take it or leave it. You have a choice. Personally, I choose to take it. I look for continual growth and development because it keeps me active and interested in life. I have encountered much in my life and find all that it has to offer can be fascinating and remarkable. Not everything that has happened to me in my life has been wonderful, but I do not regret any of it. Each stage has brought new skills and challenges, and I believe I am constantly developing from them. Now, I look forward to the next circle. As each one closes, another unlocks.

You will never know everything you need to, but you can always take something from every situation if you choose to. A marriage certificate does not come with an operator's manual. It is the same if you have children. You can read books, attend courses and try to do everything to prepare yourself for situations, but much of the learning takes place in the moment. In relationships, no two couples are the same and neither are families. We are all individuals and respond to the world in different ways. This is a good thing, by the

7: Learning and Growing

way – it makes life interesting! So much of what you learn is what you have seen in your life from your parents, experienced during your childhood, learnt from your peers and other experiences, seen on TV (unfortunately) or picked-up from books and magazines.

Consciously or unconsciously, you make choices from examples that are set before you. If you delve further into your own mind to find out what motivates you, you may learn much more, but you will still have to put it into practice.

Consider for a moment: you may understand what you want regarding feelings and emotions but, until you are faced with them, you cannot know for certainty how you will react to any given situation. You can attain skills such as how to act more rationally, with more empathy or less anger, but still get caught up in the emotion of the moment. Learning and growth is an exciting process and, for me, it certainly is a constant work in progress. The best approach is to be willing and open for change and to look at life from many angles.

Looking at life from different angles means to view yourself in different circumstances and how you behave around them. By continually learning, you are also bound to know more about the people around you. Once you understand yourself better, your relationships will improve. You will be able to decide what is working for you or not and then change those things that no longer serve you. So, how do you think that is possible?

8: Understanding People, Understanding Self

"Everything that irritates us about others can lead us to an understanding of ourselves."
– Carl Gustav Jung

I love this quote by Carl Jung, don't you? It is so true that what bothers you most about someone is what *you* most need to alter. As humans, most of us are wired to naturally engage in relationships. Certainly, some people are more outgoing and they make friends very easily. Others may be a little shy and, for them, relating is more of a challenge. But still, there is an innate tendency in most people to want to connect with others.

Unfortunately, it is not all that simple. Communication is more than just the spoken word. It is necessary; but effective communication for some, is often nonexistent. People have different personalities, perceptions and ways of communicating. This also varies for different cultures and nationalities. For instance, some people are huggers. It can be the most natural thing in the world for them to meet a complete stranger and hug them as a greeting. Others may be defensive of their personal space. No matter how well intentioned the hugger is, their way of communicating may simply not work for you if you do not like physical contact with strangers.

The Full Circle

> **Jot down how well you relate to other people, including strangers and friends**
>
> 1. Make a list **in your journal** of 10-20 people in your life and rate each individually from 1-10 as to how well you relate to them (1 being poor and 10 being fantastic).
>
> 2. Look at the traits of these people – what traits do you see in each individual that you do not like about that person? Perhaps these are the traits you display yourself.
>   - If that is the case, these traits are those you could work on for yourself.

Understanding people is important because this gives you the ability to develop better relationships. In relationships you can feel valued and needed – which is often what most of us are looking for. But to relate well, you need to have some common ground, whether it is the way you communicate, your common interests, values or lifestyle.

You are an individual. It is therefore expected that you think and act differently to other people – you already know this. You may also perceive the same situations differently. Sometimes these differences are small, which makes relating easier. It is often when these differences are truly noticeable that you will begin to struggle to communicate. If you believe everyone thinks just as you do, you may not be able to communicate effectively. What you say can mean one thing to you, yet the person you are speaking with may understand something completely different.

The way I think and feel is unique to me, just as the way you think and feel is unique to you. So too are your intentions. Understanding others is about comprehending what their intentions actually are in order to know what motivates them to make the decisions they

8: Understanding People, Understanding Self

have made. This is not a scientific principle that is defined and objective. Understanding others is subjective. When you take the time to understand others, you will be able to find out what their needs and perspectives are and how they align with yours. You will then be able to adapt how you communicate so you can be more accurately understood. You also want your needs to be heard.

Effective communication is one of the most important elements in developing successful relationships, whether these are on a personal, business or social level. Even speaking with a repair man, if your needs are not communicated correctly, the job will not be done to your satisfaction. When you are in a personal relationship with a spouse or partner, poor communication makes it difficult to lead a healthy, sustainable union.

Think about the people closest to you

1. What do you have in common?
2. How do you generally communicate with these friends and family?
   - Is this easy or more challenging for you?
3. Are there certain people that you find more difficult to interact with?
   - Can you think of a reason why this might be?

_____
_____
_____
_____
_____
_____

The Full Circle

In order to understand others, you need to develop empathy. Empathy is about seeing the world from someone else's eyes or "putting yourself in someone else's shoes". Of course, having empathy means that when you communicate with others, you can better understand what they are feeling and why they acted the way they did or said what they said. You may have been in a similar situation and get the picture of what the other person feels. When you empathise with someone, you are showing them that they are not alone at a time they might need someone most, to be there for support. Understanding others can also help in guiding you in the way you may need to move forward when interacting with them.

It is important in communication to be a good listener. Empathy, as well as understanding what the individual is actually telling you, plays a big role in this. Empathy is an advanced communication skill which many people do not possess. In my life, I have had a number of friends who have been separated and divorced. Each of them has had different circumstances around their divorces. However, I have been able to be empathetic because this is something I have experienced myself and can put myself in their shoes. When speaking with one of my friends, the conversation would most likely begin by my acknowledgement of the situation and I could say "I know how difficult this must be for you right now having gone through similar experiences when I was separated".

8: Understanding People, Understanding Self

> **Knowing how you act, react and interact with others is important**
> 1. How would you describe yourself in terms of how you are around other people?
> 2. Does who you are with impact how you interact? Does this change from person to person or group to group?
> 3. Does your level of empathy change with people you know compared with people you don't know?
> 4. Since you started discovering more about yourself, has your interaction with others changed?

_____

_____

_____

_____

_____

_____

The way you respond, and perceive others to respond, has to do with your own personal development. Once you know yourself better, you are more inclined to make the effort to get to know others better, and understanding others becomes more important. This, in turn, has the ripple effect of you having more empathy towards others. Personal development is a lifelong process without which you can become stuck in your life and less likely to develop to your full potential. If you are less aware of yourself and your motivators, you might be less likely to understand others and their motivators.

There is so much you can learn from others that will help you understand them better. You can learn about the social or cultural differences that may exist. Religious and ethnic differences, education levels and sexual orientation all play a part in the way you react, feel or communicate about a situation. Many books have been written on the differences in how men and women think and communicate and why. Authors such as Louann Brizendine, Anne Moir, David Jessel and Alan and Barbara Pease, to name a few, have written on the subject.

Men communicating with men and women to women can also vary. Certainly, you can learn from others by watching relationships and observing interactions. You have probably all seen those jokes about a woman's brain and what she is thinking in comparison to what a man is thinking in the same instance. They can be diametrically opposed; so, learning about those differences can help tremendously in building successful relationships with effective communication.

Given that each individual is different, you cannot always assume their thoughts align with each other. When you have better self-awareness, it then helps you to see how you relate outwardly to your world and those around you. This too, is like a circle. When you go inwards and become more aware of yourself, you then can look outwards and become more aware of others.

Is It That Important to Understand Ourselves?

Self-awareness, which is the ability to see who we are in our society, is one attribute of emotional intelligence. When you are more aware of your feelings, thoughts, beliefs, strengths and weaknesses, you are more likely to make changes in your behaviour. Consequently, you are more likely to be successful. When you have a clearer perception of yourself, you are better able to understand others and the way they act towards you as well.

> **Recognise how well you understand yourself**
> 1. How aware are you of your thoughts and beliefs?
> 2. Do you know what your strengths and weaknesses are? Name a few.
> 3. Are there any areas in your life in which you would like to grow?
> 4. Are there any particular areas of weakness that you desire to strengthen?
> 5. How will you feel if you develop these areas of your life?
> 6. Are you aware of any limiting beliefs that you might have?

_____
_____
_____
_____
_____
_____

One of the benefits of this self-awareness is developing more confidence which leads to setting and achieving more realistic goals. Making better choices in life includes thinking first before speaking or doing, so you avoid making an incorrect decision. You become aware that a simple change in your thoughts could make all the difference in a response. With understanding yourself comes the ability to change what you think and feel. In other words, you can change your emotional reactions.

Changing your emotions is an important step in mastering your own life and what you want from it. Essentially, the Law of Attraction happens when you understand yourself and your desires and the direction you want to take. This can be beneficial due to the fact that, if you alter your thinking and emotions, it is less likely that conflict will occur. You are attracting what you want, not what you do not want. New possibilities are now open to you.

Perhaps you may not be aware of the concept of the Law of Attraction. This states that likes attract likes and what we focus on will come to us. This is not new thinking and has come up through the ages. In the early 1900's, James Allen, a new thought writer, wrote the book *As a Man Thinketh*, and more recently many of us have heard of the book or seen the movie *The Secret* by Rhonda Byrne. Rhonda had studied many great people from history such as Plato, Newton, Beethoven, Edison and Einstein. She found that these great teachers taught us about the Law of Attraction.

The book *The Secret* features 24 new thought authors and teachers who have learnt and lived the Law of Attraction in their lives. As quoted by Bob Proctor, one of the authors in *The Secret*, "Everything that's coming into your life you are attracting into your life. And it's attracted to you by the virtue of the images you're holding in your mind. Whatever is going on in your mind you are attracting to you".

Starting Out with Self-Understanding

Start by developing a sense of self. Examine how you think and react or respond to certain situations. Are you angry, frustrated, sad or happy and what triggers those emotions? In every situation, become aware of how you feel and how you act or react. This can be difficult and confronting. You may be blissfully unaware of certain behaviours or how you respond to different situations. When faced with the reality, it may be too intimidating since you might not want to know some things about yourself, so you try to hide from them and consequently, stop evaluating.

8: Understanding People, Understanding Self

A number of years ago, I had a client who had many issues in her life. When we started to delve further into those issues as she saw them, it became very painful for her. She had hidden much of her life deep inside and bringing them to the surface was extremely upsetting. She could see that, because of these issues, her life was unhappy deep down although she put on a mask of happiness. Working through these issues allowed her to change her attitude about herself and her abilities. She could see that what she had believed all stemmed from what she believed others had said about her.

"When you start to focus on yourself and learn more about where some of your self-limiting beliefs come from, you will become aware and start believing in yourself more."
– Paulette Archer

When you examine yourself, you might start to take note of the triggers in your life. Triggers or anchors, as mentioned earlier in this book, are those things that make you easily irritated, frustrated, happy, sad or angry. When you become aware of your triggers, you can start working on ways to adapt to them or alter your behaviour so that these triggers are no longer destructive. You are more likely to be able to "talk yourself out" of a situation knowing that what you may have been telling yourself is not true and based on self-limiting beliefs. If you want to participate in a more detailed analysis, you can start a log to record your reactions to different circumstances. (Put this into your journal.)

For example, when you have a new experience, a change in your environment or when you meet new people, jot down what it felt like to experience this and how you responded. You can also put yourself into situations that are unfamiliar to you to see how you deal with them. One example would be to eat out alone at a restaurant on a Saturday night, even though this is not something you would normally do. While you are there, think about how it makes you feel to be alone surrounded by conversation and laughter. Does it make you happy, sad, lonely, or are you okay with it?

This is something I decided to do, difficult as it was at first since I never went out to dinner on my own while I was married. Now, I do enjoy it and have no problem being alone, which does occur often, especially when I am travelling by myself. By putting yourself into difficult situations, you are learning to be with yourself and becoming comfortable with it. Before you know it, you will find that it is not so frightening after all, and in time more and more situations will be comfortable for you to experience.

You can add daily thoughts into your journal about what you have experienced. You can also take into account past experiences. Think about where you have come from and the influences that have shaped you into the person you are. Were there plenty of great experiences? Was there love around you? Were you isolated or given freedom? What are your fears and emotions? Are you angry or happy with what has been your life so far? All of these things can help you discover who you are and what makes you 'tick'. Starting out on this journey may seem hard initially. However, as you start to discover more about yourself and others, it can become a very exciting journey of awareness.

> *"As you build on your knowledge you learn to understand better, love more and have greater empathy for the world around you."*
> **– Paulette Archer**

Learning never ends if you are striving to be the best you can be. Reaching your full potential in one aspect of your life tends to take you to a new level in many other areas of your life. Your thoughts of reaching a more promising future will guide you to continue your

8: Understanding People, Understanding Self

quest of personal fulfillment. Sometimes you might develop a new interest for different experiences. Like when I learnt to swim and scuba dive. This was something I never thought I would do so, when I took up the challenge, I not only acquired those skills, but I also understood a lot about me and my self-limiting beliefs.

When you finish your formal education, learning continues. If you leave school before you finish high-school, you will still be gaining knowledge on how to survive in society and you will take up new skills in order to look after yourself. Even if you have a PhD, you still do not necessarily have all the life skills required to live harmoniously with others. On some level, we will always continue to take in new information. Life's lessons can be the biggest teacher we have. If you assimilate what you experience daily, this can become a true positive in your life. If you are aware of life around you and take in each and every experience and how it affects you, you will continue to learn.

Knowledge and learning
1. Who or what do you think you learn from the most?
2. Where else can you gain knowledge?

_____

_____

_____

So, Your Values Aren't in Alignment – Who Cares?

Your values are such an important part of your life. The concept of value, as it relates to you, is something you would benefit from if you had a full understanding or conscious awareness of it. Essentially, values define who you are and what is most important for you in your life. Knowing what you value or what has value for you in life, career and relationships - in other words, both personally and professionally - helps you live with purpose.

Values are the core of your being, or what defines you as a person.

We often talk about how your values are formed from the earliest times in your life. Growing up, you get a sense of self initially from those closest to you and those who have the most influence on you. Typically, the source of your values can come from family, friends, church or religion, school, geography or demographics, economics and the media. As you get older, you may keep some of those core values but others will change as you develop as individuals. You may change your values if they no longer serve you in the achievement of your goals.

Knowing what your values are gives you more clarity about what is really important to you. This helps as you begin to make better decisions. This is because you know what you want and you strive for it. When you are living to your highest values, you tend to be happier since everything is in alignment. Once you know your values, you can keep away from those things which have a negative pull on you.

Another important reason for knowing what your core values are is, it is absolutely vital when setting goals. We talk about goals and goal setting in more detail in Chapter 9. For now, know that values have the power to determine the success or failure of your goals. If your goals are not in alignment with your values, it is more likely that you will not be motivated enough to achieve them.

Since knowing that your highest values are one of the major factors in developing your self-love and fulfilling your purpose in life, let's look at how you can identify what *your* values are. It can be easy for you to think someone else's values are yours, or

8: Understanding People, Understanding Self

you try to live by values that were taught to you by your family, teachers or peers. However, if you are not living by your own highest values, you will most probably live in conflict. Make sure you are clear about what you believe are your values so you are not living someone else's.

How do you gain clarity around knowing your values? (Take your time with the following exercise. Put this into your journal.)

1. Some things to consider before choosing your values – what do you love and what are those things you think you *should* have or do?

    a. If you believe that you should, have to or need to do something, you may be looking at the values of someone else. Consider where those thoughts have come from – perhaps your parents or family structure. Those values are not wrong or right, they just may not be what you believe is right for you. Look at what is more in alignment with how you are now as an adult. If you are living by other people's values, you are more likely to play the victim role when something is not going your way. We have spoken of this already. Write down all of those 'shoulds' and where they may have come from.

    b. Next, what do you love to do? Do you love to spend time with family or alone working on projects? Are you eager for excitement and a challenge or passionate about going to the theatre or working in your garden? With these words, you will make statements like "I love to do this or that", "This wildly excites me", "Doing this totally inspires me" or "I am eternally grateful to be doing such and such".

2. Next, jot down how you see yourself – how you identify yourself to someone. "I am a mother", "I am an accountant",

or "I am a retired librarian". You might actually be doing one thing, however, identify yourself as something else. For instance, you say you are a nurse but work in a restaurant. As you age, you identify yourself differently according to your possible values at that time. (Remember, your values will change over time.) Consider this based on each area of your life – Personal, Professional and Societal.

3. It is important for you to ask yourself a number of questions which assists in finding what those values are for you. How do you spend your time, money, energy and space? Are you organised and dependable and what types of thoughts do you most often have? Is this what you most often talk to yourself or others about? Does anything inspire you and is this what you read about or study? Do you set goals and, if so, what sorts were the ones which stand out for you when accomplished? In this list, see what repeats itself. You will need to summarise and prioritise the words according to how often each one comes up.

4. You might find by asking yourself these questions there is a central theme, maybe words that repeat themselves. For example, I might say "I love people", "I enjoy volunteering and helping people" or "meeting people from all walks of life is a passion for me". The word "people" comes out regularly so my value may be helping others, helping society or volunteering. Record these comments to pick repeating words. Again, it is necessary to summarise and prioritise the words according to how often each one comes up.

5. Ask yourself these above questions several times until you have a list of words for each question. Also, what are three ways you spend most of your time. You can name more than

8: Understanding People, Understanding Self

three but may find three will be predominant. Or what types of books do you spend your time reading? What are the titles of the last three books you have read? Is there a central theme here?

6. From the above series of words, you will come up with a preliminary register of values. What you have just created is random and is your initial list. Deciding on your values hierarchy shows which values are the most important to you. If you were to look at education and learning, you may see one show up more often than the other when making out your list. The word that shows up the most would be first. (The values hierarchy is an expression of your character which is especially important when setting goals.)

7. Next, order the values with number 1 being the most important. This is your revised list. You can look over the initial list and see what appeals to you most and reorder the values. You can also look at two at a time which resonate with you and then ask yourself, "which is the most important to me if I had to choose between the two?".

8. Imagine you end up with ten values. Fine tune these ten to get your top five. This then becomes the values you live by. By knowing this, you are better able to shape your life based on knowing what it is you are most in alignment with.

To reach a better understanding of what your values are, you can take a look at the following compilation of words – which is certainly not exhaustive. You may see many of the words you used in the exercises. Feel free to add your own values to this list. Take note, those with the asterisks could be considered the real core values which most people might have.

It is possible to have a different set of values for each area of your life – that is, personal, business and within the societal context.

The Full Circle

- *Abundance
- *Accountability
- *Achievement
- Advancement and Promotion
- *Adventure
- Affection (love and caring)
- Affluence
- *Ambition
- Appreciation
- Approval
- Assertiveness
- Arts
- Authority
- Authenticity
- *Awareness
- *Balance
- Being active
- *Beauty
- Bravery
- Candor
- Capability
- Charisma
- *Cheerfulness
- *Clarity
- Cleanliness
- Close relationships
- *Comfort
- Commitment
- *Compassion
- Communication
- Competence
- *Connection
- Consistency
- Contentment
- *Contribution
- Cooperation
- *Courage
- *Creativity
- Credibility
- *Curiosity
- Democracy
- Financial Independence
- *Flexibility
- *Freedom
- *Friendships
- Frugality
- *Fulfilment
- *Fun
- Generosity
- Growth
- *Happiness
- *Harmony
- *Health
- *Honesty
- *Honour
- *Humility
- Humour
- *Independence
- Inner harmony
- *Integrity
- *Intellectual status
- *Intimacy
- Justice
- *Kindness
- Leadership
- Leisure activity
- *Liveliness
- Living life to the fullest
- Longevity
- *Love
- Loyalty
- Making a difference
- Meaningful work
- Merit
- Mindfulness
- Motivation
- *Money
- *Nature
- Openness
- Organisation
- Partnership
- *Passion
- *Simplicity
- Sincerity
- Solitude
- *Spirituality
- *Spontaneity
- *Stability
- *Status
- *Strength
- Structure
- *Success
- *Teamwork
- Temperance
- Thoughtfulness
- *Tolerance
- *Traditionalism
- Tranquility
- Travel
- Trust
- *Truth
- Understanding
- Uniqueness
- Virtue
- *Vitality
- Volunteering
- *Wealth
- *Wisdom
- Work ethic
- Worthiness

8: Understanding People, Understanding Self

As an example, your lists may look something like this:

Your initial list:	Revised list:	Reordered final five values:
Family/Friends	Family and friends	1. Physical fitness
Success/Achievement	Achievement	2. Honesty
Determination/Perseverance	Perseverance	3. Financial independence
Health/Physical fitness	Physical fitness	4. Family and friends
Responsibility	Education	5. Leisure
Education	Leisure	
Leisure activity/Happiness	Financial independence	
Commitment	Fulfillment	
Work ethic/Financial independence	Personal development	
Fulfillment	Honesty	
Personal development		
Honesty		

This now shows the values you live by as: Physical fitness, Honesty, Financial independence, Family and friends and Leisure.

There is so much more to consider with values, since they are a very important measure for how well you are able to live your life and fulfill your dreams. They are also significant in how you get on with other people. In life, you get to meet different people with different backgrounds and belief systems.

When communicating with others, if the values of those people are very different from yours, it may be difficult to have a meaningful relationship with them. You will be seeking out relationships and individuals, based on the sorts of values you are drawn to. If honesty and/or integrity is one of your core values, it would be difficult for you to maintain a meaningful relationship with a cheater who follows no moral code. You will not be attracted to those people who do not fulfill your specific needs and who go against your beliefs.

Being 'At Cause' Or 'At Effect' Rears Its Head Once Again!

It is very important to understand the concept of being 'at cause' and 'at effect' as it reflects all aspects of your life. Learning about yourself gives you the understanding as to why you think and do what you do. If you understand this, you will know that, for each individual, the same holds true. Diverse reactions can be expected and you need not blame someone for a reaction which is not the same as yours. You can simply accept that people are different. You can endeavour to understand them, but it does not always mean the way you relate or communicate with each other will be the same.

Understanding Self or Others, Is This the Chicken or The Egg?

There is always another circle to follow. And as a circle can start and finish at different points, it may be difficult to decide which comes first, understanding yourself or others. No matter what, understanding is just the beginning of the journey. It can simply take you to an advanced level of awareness.

In life, many new situations are bound to come up from time to time, and the possibility exists that there will always be situations that you have not faced in the past. At times in your life, change can be ushered in by getting married, or not; having a family or being childless; getting a new job or retiring. Life may throw curve balls at you and the circumstances you thought you would be in for a while, may change. It may be hard to understand yourself. However, looking at how you react to different circumstances gives you an insight. Understanding others can help you understand yourself and vice versa. If you were to get divorced, lose a loved one, a job, a home, get sick or handicapped, you may be experiencing something completely new to you.

All of these situations can challenge you on different levels than where you have been before, and your self-awareness gives you the ability to tackle each situation in the best way possible. Understanding the way other people have coped can help you cope. Taking lessons from those who have gone before you can teach you how best to look at the changes you are now experiencing. The more you understand yourself, the more you are bound to understand others.

Awareness and inspiration

1. Have you experienced a new level of awareness at some point in your life? How did it come about and how did it make you feel?

2. Who inspires you? It can be someone you know or don't know – perhaps someone famous. What is it about them that you find inspiring?

3. Have you ever inspired someone else? How would it feel if you were to be the inspiration for others?

_____
_____
_____
_____
_____

The Full Circle

There are many famous people who serve as inspiration for others. However, I often find that it is the ordinary unassuming people who inspire me most. Age and experience of the individual does not matter either – some of my best lessons have come from my children, especially when they were quite young. I learn lessons all the time from the people with whom I interact because I am curious. Curious about my surroundings – how and why certain things have come to pass. What I have also come to appreciate is that a lot of people couldn't care less, and cannot understand why 'it' matters, whatever the 'it' is. They just let life pass them by without making any changes, whether for better or worse.

Funny thing is, at a point in my life, I was just like that. If it did not affect me, I didn't care. And if it did in a negative way, I felt powerless to change. Now I acknowledge that for me, this is not what it is about. There is more to my journey than sitting around waiting for "life to happen". It is about having interests, being inquisitive, asking questions and thinking about the world around me. It is about setting goals based on what I want at the present moment and into the future. This keeps my mind active and I can reflect on my life, make sense out of it and come to the realisation that, without everything that has happened to me, I would not have been myself. I wouldn't change that for anything. Every experience, whether good or bad, has made me who I am. Without them I would not be Paulette Archer, the person sitting here writing a book she never thought was possible.

If my life is truly about setting goals around what I want now and into the future, then it would be a good idea to look at the real value of goals. Perhaps for you it will help in deciding whether this will be the same.

9: What is the Real Value of Goals?

"What you get by achieving your goals is not as important as what you become by achieving your goals."
— **Henry David Thoreau**

Even before you consciously think about setting and achieving goals, you are actually doing just that. In your early developmental years of life, you set out to crawl, walk and then run. As you get older, you learn to talk, read and write, finish school, get a job and so on. Some of those activities you do not consciously set out to achieve, like walking and talking. It is something you naturally learn as you develop. You may not even be aware of it, but even at a young age you simply do things that reflect what you want in life. You want to play, so you learn to walk and run. You want to communicate, so you learn to talk. Essentially, that is what goals are about – achieving your ideal future.

List a goal or goals you are working toward right now
 1. What is it/are they?

_____

_____

Recognising the Usefulness of Setting Goals

I first became aware of goal setting many years ago, but I never did much about formally initiating it until more recently. In the past, I would think of what I wanted in life, however, I never set it down as a goal. New Year's resolutions were the closest I came to goal setting. Of course, I would start the year off with them, but since I did not put any effort in, they were short-lived and, in the end, not accomplished. This could be the same for many of you. The first time I really had to think about what I wanted in life was when I was finishing high school. After graduating, I set the goal to go to university and study nursing. Another more subconscious goal at that time was to work as a nurse, eventually get married and have children.

During my active work years, I had objectives around what type of job I desired and where I wanted to work. I think what is more significant now is that I have consciously set and achieved many more goals over the last decade than previously. I have come to appreciate the value of goals and how to set those that I can and will achieve. When setting goals, it is important to set realistic ones. I will talk more on this later.

The experience of formally setting goals and achieving them has been wonderful and has encouraged me to keep on setting both short and long-term ones. These can change and are altered from time to time. The important thing is that they are helping me achieve what I really want in life. By living within my values, I am setting realistic goals and, therefore, I am far more likely to achieve them.

9: What is the Real Value of Goals?

> **You and goal setting**
>
> 1. Are you in the habit of setting goals?
> 2. Do you think goal setting is important? Why or why not?
> 3. What, for you, is the mark of a realistic goal?
> 4. Have you ever set out to achieve a specific goal? How did you go about reaching it? How did it feel to attain it?
> 5. What do you think would be different in your life if you had goals that you were specifically and consistently working towards?

_____
_____
_____
_____
_____
_____
_____

Goal setting can be for everyone. However, not everyone thinks this way. For many, you have some idea of what you want in life, but you may not take any deliberate steps towards it. You simply let life happen and see what turns out.

If you do not get to where you thought you wanted to go in life, there are always reasons why things have not worked out. If this is the case, you may give excuses such as: "I wanted to retire when I was 40, but because of the economic downturn I couldn't" or "I wanted to go to university but couldn't afford to". I have to question what you have done to achieve these goals. Did you

The Full Circle

actually do anything to attain them or did you simply expect them to come to pass?

You will not achieve anything unless you set your mind to it and take the necessary steps toward it. Luck can only take you part of the way. Even all of the hype about the "Laws of Attraction" does not work by thinking alone. Gary Player, a championship golfer, was once asked if luck had anything to do with his success. His answer was: "I find the more I practice, the luckier I get". In other words, success has far less to do with luck and much more to do with effort.

> **Luck**
> 1. How much of your success to date has been about luck?
> 2. If someone were to give you a lucky charm where your efforts were guaranteed to succeed, would you be inclined to put in more effort or less effort?

_____
_____
_____
_____
_____

We often hear the stories of individuals who wanted something so much that they achieved it under great adversity. What makes this possible? Is it because they want 'that thing' so badly? Or their burning desire for 'that thing' prompted them to pour out all effort to achieve it? When challenges happen, many people give up. However, for others, challenges are merely motivators to push

9: What is the Real Value of Goals?

even harder to achieve their targets. These people have a mindset of "I will do what it takes to reach this goal. I will make it". With this winning mindset, they press on and are able to surmount all obstacles in their path of reaching those set goals.

When you have achieved your goals, you have attained success. Whenever I contemplate setting goals, I use the acronym I CREATE SUCCESS. To make sure that my goal has all the required components, I use the acronym CREATE, which I will explain shortly. My acronym for SUCCESS is:

S – Self-Belief

U – Understanding (your values)

C – Clarity (around where you are heading)

C – Celebrate (your success)

E – Empowerment

S – Stretch (yourself)

S – Stay (on track)

Taking action is a vital element of achieving goals. It seems that doing this as a regular practice occurs more often with highly successful individuals. These individuals do not just talk or dream about what they want out of life, they find ways to make it happen. Setting goals is one tool that assists high achievers turn dreams into reality.

There are many benefits attached to goal setting. For one, being able to see what in your life is really important to you enables you to develop a clear idea of where to place your values. Through this, you can focus on those areas of your life that are lacking – personally or professionally. In the process, you become more aware of your strengths and weaknesses. This can, in turn, help you to make better life decisions.

The Full Circle

When you are goal setting, you are looking at the priorities in your life – what you value and what is important to you. It can lead to a better self-image. When you take more responsibility for what happens in your life, you are not leaving life up to chance. Goals definitely help keep you on track and more focused on the outcome. If you are consistently working with a clear focus, you are shielded from wasting time on meaningless tasks. The goals help to keep you on course. A clearer personal vision can be possible and you can develop a sense of success once the objective is achieved.

The Goal Achieving Journey

Both achieving goals and the journey to that end are equally important. By starting out with an intention, you are comparing your life as it is at that moment to what you want it to be in the future. The process then empowers you to take steps to execute the goal. This may involve making changes or learning new skills – which, in itself, gives you a sense of accomplishment because you are taking control of your life by learning and growing. You are being responsible for what is happening in your life. The little steps along the way mean you are getting closer to your dream.

This is why it is vastly important to celebrate each little win in your overall quest. By setting goals, you are taking an active part in your life each step of the way. It is these small victories that bring your desires to fruition - and perhaps those that you once thought impossible. As each step is completed, it places you in a more positive frame of mind.

9: What is the Real Value of Goals?

> **Effort, work and achievement**
>
> 1. When someone talks about effort, what feelings come to mind?
>
> 2. Do you sigh at the thought of work or get excited at the prospect of getting involved in a project? Are you a big dreamer or cautious in your ambitions? What do you think the advantages and drawbacks of each approach are?
>
> 3. Have you ever looked back and realised how much you have learnt in the process of achieving a goal? How have you been able to apply that to other areas of your life?
>
> 4. What do you think is the most achievable goal you could set for yourself right now? Will the goal stretch you or will it be easy to reach? How much are you motivated to achieve it?
>
> 5. Have you ever given up on a goal? Why do you think you gave up?

_____
_____
_____
_____
_____
_____
_____

You may often hear people say "Dream big! Anything is possible!". This may well be true; nevertheless, there are a few things to keep in mind. Dreaming big can be of value as long as you are realistic

The Full Circle

with your intention and time frame. You also need to think about your abilities. You may not know everything you need to achieve your goal. That is okay. Part of the journey is the learning. Just keep in mind how much you will need to learn and how long it may take.

A medical student does not become a surgeon overnight. He or she studies for years, serves internships and has to practice in the area of specialisation under another doctor for some time before he can operate independently. It involves a great amount of dedication and, for someone who dreams of being a surgeon, it is not an impossible dream. The goal is set knowing full well what is involved and the dedication is there to achieve it.

To a large extent, knowing what you want out of life means you understand how hard you are willing to work to this end. You know how easily you may give up. When commencing, be realistic. Begin with steps you know are achievable. Then, once you have ticked them off, you can start to raise the bar.

You do not go to the start line of a marathon without putting in some kilometres on the road. If you do, you are likely to injure yourself or collapse and have to give up. The same applies to goal setting. If you want to run a marathon, you practice by starting with 5 kms then 10 kms and building up to half marathons. Once you are running comfortably, and have a good level of fitness, you can start running faster and further. Suddenly, your thoughts of running a marathon can become a realistic and achievable goal.

Yet, when you started out, it may have seemed like a big impossible dream, but the smaller targets along the way help you to build up to the 'big one' at the end. Goals that are just fancy dreams and have no stepping stones to help you get there may not be achieved. This may be because you genuinely do not have the required ability or are just not willing to put in the time or effort to change.

A positive mindset is invaluable in achieving goals. This is why milestones are so important. They give you something to celebrate along the journey. Often, if you do not think they are possible, you can get discouraged and give up before you even try to succeed. You may get frustrated or overwhelmed because you are not making the progress you want. If your goal is too big, you may even avoid it and, rather work on something else that is easier to accomplish. This is a clear indicator that maybe you need to break the goal down into bite-sized chunks. Go back to the small steps, so that getting there is more realistic. Have you ever heard the phrase, "How do you eat an elephant?". The answer is "One bite at a time".

On the opposite end of the spectrum, goals that are too small may not motivate you sufficiently. While goals need to be realistic, they also need to stretch you and take you outside of your comfort zone – that is where the learning and growth takes place.

What Makes the Impossible, Possible?

You may often hear of situations in life where a totally unrealistic goal was achieved. What is it that brings the impossible dream to reality? Some people say that if you do not try, you will never know. Is it just about trying or is it much more than that?

A characteristic of many successful people is that they are driven. They set their sights on what they aspire to, put their lives into gear and then go full steam ahead to achieve it. Characteristics such as determination and perseverance have a major impact. If a goal is really massive, there is often a sense of learning, experimenting or growing. It is about expanding your world and rising up to meet the challenge. There is also a willingness to improve and strive for a better life. A willingness and motivation to do and be responsible for what you have in your life.

The Full Circle

> **More thoughts on goal setting for you**
> 1. How much does who you are impact on your ability to achieve your goals?
> 2. What do you think can make the difference in you achieving your goals or not?
> 3. What benefits are there in goal setting?
> 4. How will you feel if you are living a life where you are consistently achieving your goals?

_____
_____
_____
_____
_____

Guidelines for Goal Setting

My starting point is to first consider if it is a long or short-term goal. Next is to think about the goal itself. What outcome do I want and is it something that motivates me? Since they are aligned to your values, it makes sense to understand that setting them will mean doing what you love. In this event you are more likely to succeed. If I set goals that are not that important to me, or that I see no value in, I am less likely to put in the effort needed to bring them to fruition. I have seen this happen more than once in my life.

You may ask "Why set a goal that isn't important to you"? In life, you may choose to learn a new skill – let's consider learning to play bridge. This was something I wanted to do, so I initiated lessons.

9: What is the Real Value of Goals?

My parents and many of my friends played bridge and I thought it would be great to be able to share this hobby with them. I fulfilled the series of classes on two different occasions; however, I never learned to play. I did not feel a failure because of it. Instead, I knew bridge was just not for me.

I took up scuba diving instead, which none of my bridge friends did. The same thing can happen when you chose a career to go into. By the time you finish your studies, you may find this is just not for you. You still have a choice – you can move onto something different at the time or work towards doing something else when time and/or money permits. Many years ago, a friend joined the navy only to find that he had suffered intractable seasickness. This did not end his career there however – he became a navy pilot instead!

Sometimes I set several smaller goals that build on one another in order to get to another stage. In this case, I will look at the order of progression as well as the ultimate goal. Building a house without the foundation will not work. If I need to gain a certain qualification before I can achieve a goal around my profession, for instance, then I will need to take those steps first. Also, I need to prioritise so that I will be confident I am not setting too many at a time. Too many goals may not be achievable because I could lose focus and possibly become overwhelmed. This is something I am often guilty of because I have a tendency to want to do more, so I take on a lot in my enthusiasm and then later get overwhelmed.

A key step is that, once I have thought through and made the decision on my goal, I write it down. To ensure my goal has all the required components I use the acronym CREATE to set it up. (When you use the CREATE method to set up your goal, the planning is straightforward.)

C – I want to be Clear and Concise about what my goal is. This way there will be no confusion about what I am wanting to achieve.

R – Am I **R**ealistic when setting that goal? Can it be achieved? If it is too easy then the satisfaction of reaching it could be anticlimactic, and if it is too hard it may be demoralising if not reached. I endeavour to make it challenging, yet **R**ealistic and **R**ewarding when reached. For instance: using weight loss as an example works well because many of us have this in mind. If I had 30 kgs. to lose, it is going to take time. It will not happen overnight, so I would not set the goal to achieve this in a short space of time; otherwise, I might get overwhelmed too easily and be doomed for failure. A better way would be to plan on losing ten kgs. within certain time frames until I had lost 30 kgs.

E – My goal must be **E**cological. In other words, it should be something that is good for me, you and the universe. It needs to be nondestructive and positive. In the weight loss example, not eating for a week and totally starving myself is not ecological. I still need to eat, I just have to alter how I am eating.

A – My goal should be in the present, or **A**s now. When I write it down, I therefore state it in present tense, as if it has **A**lready happened. This allows me to visualise it as having occurred.

T – My goal should be **T**oward what I want and **T**imed, so a date is put to it. When I set up my goal I put the date that it is achieved. Open ended goals may never be achieved.

E – And lastly, I need **E**vidence that it has been reached so there is the timing for when it is complete and writing down what I am doing when this goal has been achieved.

In the planning stage, if there are a number of steps to be taken, document each one. It may take many little steps in order to reach the final stage. One of the most important aspects of goal setting is to set exact limits in terms of milestones. In the weight loss example, I may look at losing the 30 kgs. in six months.

In order to achieve this, I will have to do something different to my normal lifestyle and routine. I would first make a plan about how I was going to get the weight down. I might do a daily meal plan, calorie count or portion control. I might consider the type of exercise regime that I would implement and set a schedule. I might sign up with a weight loss coach to help me. None of these things happen without taking action. Then, I would break down the kg per week loss so that I could get to the 30 kgs. in six months.

Each milestone to get to the end step must be measurable in terms of time frames and amounts, so that the degree of success can be measured. The last consideration is to evaluate the goal within a personal context. Is it relevant to me and my life and where I want to be heading? In other words, does it fit into the bigger picture for my life? Does it align with my highest values, interests and ambitions?

The Full Circle

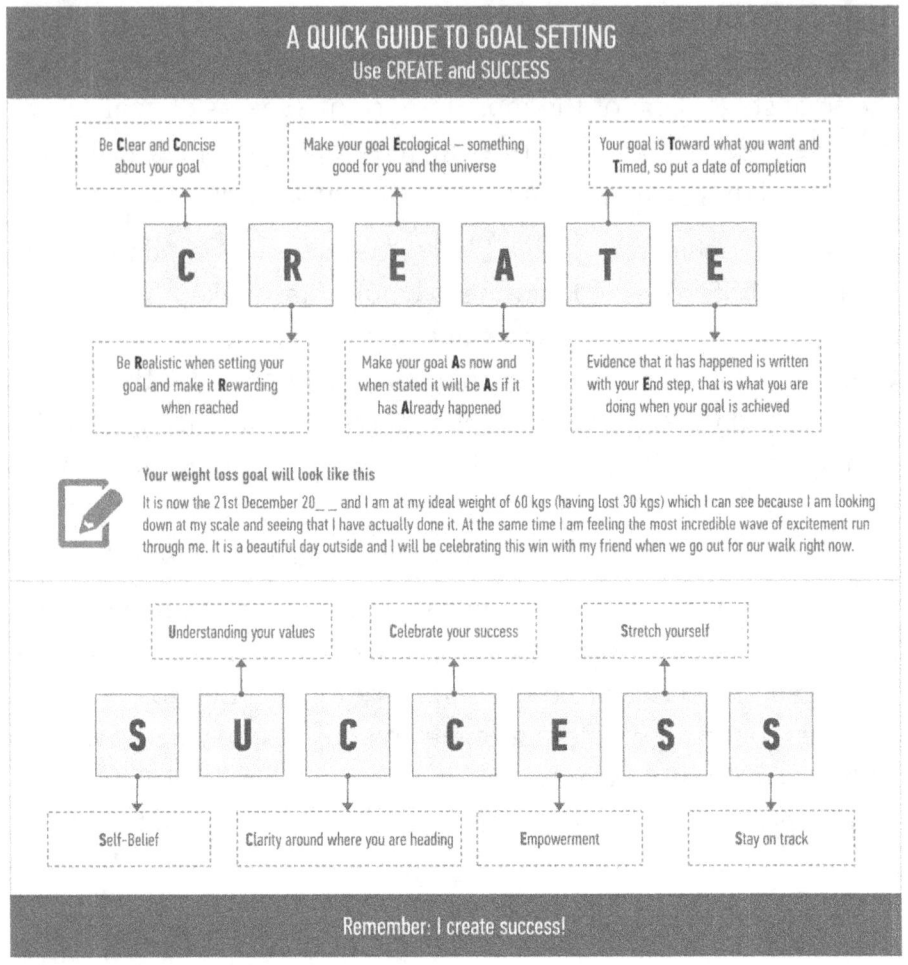

Can the Goal Posts Change?

It is important to understand that goals are dynamic and strategic. In the same way as business strategies may be reviewed and adapted midway into it, so too goals may need to be reviewed, adjusted or just changed, or even sometimes, deleted! Just because you do not achieve one goal does not necessarily mean the effort has been a failure. There is so much you learn as part of the journey, as you have seen with my friend who joined the Navy.

9: What is the Real Value of Goals?

Because success and achievement have always been important to me, this is a view that has changed in my own life. Nowadays, if a goal is not met, I look at the learning that has come from it more than the fact that I have not achieved it. What I mean here is that, if I evaluate what the purpose was and look at it realistically, I may find that I set unrealistic time frames or dollar figures to it. Perhaps my life has changed and so this goal is no longer relevant to what I am doing now. It could be that I simply lost momentum in reaching it, therefore, it was not achieved. Perhaps I will consider my intention for the goal and say, "I did not achieve this because I did nothing to work towards achieving it". This then is an opportunity to re-evaluate.

I have had a number of goals in recent years that have not been attained due to my back and nerve damage issues. I have not been physically able to get out and do as much as I had in the past. I set fitness goals around my physical abilities as they had been, however, are unrealistic in the place I am now. At first this was very hard for me, both emotionally and physically. Consequently, I overdid my exercise which led to further concerns. I did lapse a few times before I finally accepted my physical constraints, and now I am more realistic when setting those fitness goals. Perhaps you have a similar condition that you are struggling with?

Occasionally I do not achieve a goal because it has not aligned with my values. It is difficult to motivate myself when this is the case. I know in my past, when I was working in our family business, I desired so much to do a great job and be part of the everyday decision making. I wanted to learn and do what I could. I only worked when I was needed in the business, therefore, I was not there consistently and often lost the flow. I was not made to feel a real part of the business either, since I was not included when it came to decision making. Consistency and commitment- two of my values, were not being met. I was unsuccessful in achieving my goals around my work at that time

The Full Circle

If I have not reached a goal, I can review what effort I took or did not take and why. Since action needs to occur before it is achieved, if I have not taken steps in a forward direction, nothing will happen. Once I have evaluated the goal, I may see that the techniques I used to achieve it were not effective. Perhaps my plan for executing it was not clear enough and I was too easily distracted by other things in my life. If this is the case, I need to question the importance of that specific goal.

Initially, after my last divorce, I set a number of goals I did not achieve. My failure here was that I was trying to do too much and became overwhelmed. I wanted many things to happen in a short space of time, so I was destined to failure. Some of the things I wanted to do were taking a few courses I thought I might enjoy. This was to increase my skill set so that I would have something to enable me to find work. I found those goals did not interest me enough, so were totally abandoned.

For the goals that I did not achieve, on reflection, I realised that they were either unrealistic, not in line with my values or did not hold enough interest. I initially felt as if I had failed. However, later when I discovered more about the best way to set goals, I could see that they served as a learning experience for me and I no longer dwell on the "what ifs".

9: What is the Real Value of Goals?

> **Recognise a goal you have achieved which has made a big impact on your life**
> 1. What was the goal?
> 2. What has that impact been?
> 3. How has it changed your life or your mindset?
> 4. Do you have a goal now that you dream of achieving that could potentially change your life? What is it and how will it change your life?

_____
_____
_____
_____
_____
_____

Wow, I Did It!

There are a few goals that I have achieved which made a big impact on my life. These include learning to water and snow ski, as well as learning to swim and scuba dive. Graduating from university with a Bachelor of Science Degree and becoming a successful nurse were in my sights since leaving high school and achieving them gave me a real sense of accomplishment. Having two wonderful children was certainly a goal that I achieved despite the difficulties I went through before they were born.

In more recent years, realising my dream of becoming a life coach and successful business owner was also a great achievement for me. I know the reason they made such an impact on my life is because of the effort I put into achieving them. They were something *I* strived for and was not doing for someone else. They were also aligned with my values, which makes all the difference – as you have seen.

There were times that some of these goals seemed like an impossible dream. However, by putting in persistent determined effort, I was able to succeed despite the limiting beliefs I may have had along the way, as well as any obstacles which arose. A number of years ago, I was a co-author of another book and, when the deadlines were assigned, I found myself in hospital. Quite a bit of what I wrote at that time was while lying in a hospital bed in pain and on heavy medication. Yet, I was not late with the completion of each deadline. I accomplished that goal and was elated that I had done so under such conditions.

I may have originally set some goals around the suggestion of others, which was the case with learning to water ski and snow ski. I find it interesting and exciting to consider doing something that I had never envisaged and being successful at it. Perhaps you will be able to set some goals for yourself now which will be the start of a happier you. Having something to aim for is rewarding and satisfying.

Learning to be single again and loving my life after many years in relationships was a goal I reached in spite of myself. I questioned whether I could be on my own and survive. I didn't know if I could be on my own without being lonely. When I look back now, I see that this time was a huge learning curve for me. To think I even thought I could not survive alone seems ridiculous enough. Yet, when I was first on my own, and even when I was still in the relationship, the thought of being alone was frightening enough to keep me there. You may have had similar thoughts and, if so, set one small goal right now which will take you out of your comfort zone and ultimately, to discovering it is indeed possible to function on your own.

9: What is the Real Value of Goals?

If you are just coming out of a relationship or are newly on your own for whatever reason, avoid the temptation of jumping into another relationship too soon. Learn to love yourself and enjoy your own company first. My goal of finding happiness again was independently achieved, and I believe that the steps I took to set goals and change my life were instrumental in this. By setting goals and achieving them, I developed a sense of being a winner in life. As a result, my life is much more positive. I look at designing the life I choose as opposed to that of someone else. What could be more perfect?

The type of goals I have had over the years has changed. Now, I am more inclined to set goals around myself and what I want to achieve, rather than goals that include being a wife or mother. I believe many of the goals I had in the past were based on what someone else in my life was doing. My goals were therefore, based on the hope that the other person would be successful. I also did not set goals which were time based and specific. Much of the time I was living at effect, and goals did not feature very strongly for me. I really did not choose what I wanted in life but, rather, just let it happen.

Sometimes I have adjusted my already set goals and I am okay with this. I think it is important to look at them and make sure I am on course in achieving them. If I am off-track, I can readjust and change course. This may mean that I might not have set them realistically enough in the first place, and so, when I take another look, I can see why I have wavered from the end step.

One goal that I altered was finishing this book. I had originally set a time frame to finish, which in the wider scheme of things was impossible. I had actually set several at the same time and was not focused equally on anything – let alone everything I wanted to do. The good thing is that I still achieved my goal of writing the book - that is why you are reading it now - just a bit later than planned. I saw close to my time frame that this was not going to happen. Rather than stressing about it, I simply gave myself more time. Another reason that this book took me longer is because, once I started writing, I was doing more healing. Sometimes my thoughts brought up the past that I had not been thinking about and it was confronting for me. I needed to take time out from the writing. This was not given any consideration when I set my goal.

At the same time I began writing, I had set a business goal – which I did not achieve. Once again, I could see a realistic time frame was not set. All the factors I needed in order to accomplish it were not contemplated. Here, poor planning was the reason I was not making headway with the goal. This brought home to me, once again, the importance of being specific and realistic when setting goals. In both cases, I did not throw away the goals; I just had to have more realistic expectations and time frames. Setting two enormous goals at the same time was overwhelming and unrealistic for me.

Getting into the goal setting mindset is important before setting a goal. I ask myself questions such as: How important is it to me? What will it be like when I have achieved the goal? How will it look and feel? What will I feel like if I don't achieve it? How long has this been an issue for me, how long have I wanted to achieve it and what has stopped me in the past? Do I really want it? I keep my goal in the forefront of my mind and I have affirmations around my goals and say them daily to remind myself what I need to be focused on.

Goals are important to keep us on track with our life dreams and desires. When you are successful in achieving your goals, it can give you a sense of accomplishment and prosperity. It is important when you have achieved your goal to celebrate your win. This is a valuable step in the goal setting process. Goals keep us focused on what we truly want out of life and help us to stretch ourselves so we can reach and discover more of our true potential.

The concept of reward is something that has not come naturally to me. My parents were not the type of people who would give me a treat if I behaved well or was successful at something. There were never any comments made such as "if you do well you can have a new toy". We were expected to do our best rather than doing our best because of what we may receive. Once I had children, I followed suit.

As an adult, thinking of rewarding myself for an achievement or success was foreign to me. When I started my journey of self-development, I learnt about the idea of celebrating my wins when I accomplished something. Now, when I set a goal and there is something I want, I have to stop myself from just going out and getting it. I take a step back and remember that the bonus comes when I have achieved my goal, not now. This can simply be a trip to the mountains, or a walk by the sea – it does not have to be anything material or expensive. Just the concept of reward or celebration gives a different meaning of working towards a goal.

If I am visualising what I want and see myself reaching the goal, I know in that same picture my reward for the effort will come about. It brings new and stronger meaning to the goal. If I were to have exactly what I want at any given time, I might not even feel the need to set goals. What would be the point? Now, in rewarding myself, it is almost like achieving two goals for the price of one! To have a goal and achieve it is a wonderful feeling. The reward is just the icing on the cake. Plus, getting a reward pays tribute to my accomplishments – like a trophy won in a competition.

When you reach your goals, you normally would expect to feel a strong sense of fulfillment. It is excellent if you achieve what you set out to do earlier than planned, but I feel outstanding even when I reach my goal later than planned. At least I have achieved it. I did not give up. I took steps to do it and can be proud of myself for accomplishing it. I would imagine most people would feel the same about achievement. When something is handed to you on a plate, it is a lot less meaningful than when you play an active role in its completion.

The Full Circle

Goals are very important now in my circle of life and, as I have shown here, the circles repeat themselves as each new goal is set. It is an easy plan to follow and can be immensely rewarding. Once the circle of the goal is complete, a new one can commence – there is no need to change the structure to set the goal. I love my CREATE formula and hope you will give it a try and find success for yourself.

> *"Want change in your life? Create goals around your values to create success."*
> **– Paulette Archer**

So, what is the main reason for setting goals? The answer, in summary, is to have success which, of course, means many different things to many people. Let's have a look at success and see what it can mean for you. Will you achieve it if you set goals based on your true values?

10: Success

"I don't measure a man's success by how high he climbs but how high he bounces when he hits bottom."
– George S. Patton

There are innumerable definitions for success. It could be said that success is defined on a very personal level. Success is not the same for any two people. Success can be elusive and intangible. It is subjective because the way I perceive something is different from the way you do. One person's success can be another person's failure, or only partial success. So, how is success really measured?

What does success mean to you?

By definition, success can be a way of determining social status, or it can be a measure of one's achievements or goals. Success generally means something that has been acquired with a favourable outcome. Success can be measured in terms of one's life or career accomplishments. For some, success can be attaining wealth, a particular position in life, a profession, an honour or award.

The Full Circle

Recognition, fame or respect can be essential components of success for some. Yet, even these things are subjective. A vast amount of wealth for one individual could be pocket change for another. If you have a conversation about success, some of the common responses include finding a dream job or being in a happy relationship. For others, success is having money or power, being an elite sportsman or being a parent. If we were to talk to individuals in a third world country, success may be having enough food to feed their family each day or keeping their family safe.

If you consider all of these things, perhaps success does not lie in an isolated incident, thing or achievement. Rather, it works a continual journey into our lives where we work towards those things that are important to us. Could success be defined by whatever you want it to be? I believe so.

My personal measures of success are both qualitative and quantitative. Qualitatively, I measure success based on my level of happiness or contentment in life. It is about my inner journey. This is not something that I can measure definitively but, rather, it is a feeling that I have when I have accomplished something that I set out to achieve. Sometimes it is about what I have done to change my life for the better and how I have grown and developed over the years. In a way, it is my happiness monitor. The additional personal measures of success are more difficult to assess because they are gauged by how I feel inside. This is qualitative in nature.

10: Success

> **Make note of your top five measures of success**
> 1. Have these measures changed as you have matured?
> 2. How do you think your standards differ from those of other people around you?

_____

_____

_____

_____

Quantitative success can be appraised. As an example, consider our goal around weight loss. When it is achieved, the kg amount lost can be calculated and you can see you have been successful. When I have finished a project within a certain time frame or have reached a financial target, this means success. I have set goals around my career and, once again, when I have accomplished those I will have been successful. My measures will differ based on what it is I am looking to achieve. These are the more tangible areas of success for me. I can put a number or time figure on these things, they can be computed and the success of the goal is evident.

Nowadays, I feel successful in my life because what I am doing is more in alignment with my values. I am happier within myself. That is success to me. My measure of success changes according to the area of life in which the goals are set. As a broad definition, to be truly successful means that in all areas of my life, I am functioning to my full capacity; and I am happy and content.

In the Resources at the end of the book on page 256, I will go through an exercise called the *Lifestyle Circle* which gives an indication of how well balanced your life is. By viewing this, you will be able to see what areas are lacking and you will also see

The Full Circle

those areas in which you have had success, particularly if they rank highly. If I am spending more time on one area of my life than others, something is bound to be neglected. By looking at the Lifestyle Circle, I can clearly see where I can even up my life so that it becomes more balanced if, in fact, there are areas which could be lacking. To have a balanced lifestyle is personal success for me and one I regularly tweak so that it eventuates.

> **You and success**
>
> 1. Do you think success can emerge from failure? Explain how.
> 2. Is success the end goal or just a starting point or step up to the next level?
> 3. Can success happen unexpectedly?

_____

_____

_____

_____

_____

Success builds on itself in a way. When I am positive and happy, success is automatic. There will always be situations that occur which will give me success in my future. Whether they are from reaching a goal I have strived for or simply by having a happy and fulfilled life. Success, for me, is also about how I can impact the lives of others so they, too, can achieve 'success' in their life.

There is no timeline to success. As my life goes through its various circles, each movement presents new challenges to overcome and new goals to reach. It can be a full circle, as it were. I can come back to the beginning and start all over, but the next time the beginning is at a different level from the first. Like that onion which has layers. Each new layer leads to a new level of success. I can, with each new goal, strive for a little bit more and get out of my comfort zone, yet again. When I do, this is when I have the biggest 'wins'. It is not just about the dream of success, but about the ACTION that goes into making it possible.

As I carry on down my path of personal development, I will continue to grow in order to assist more individuals to find their purpose and become successful themselves. As I get older, the intangible successes mean more to me than they did previously. Besides my personal success, such as having more time with my family, enjoying life and having financial security, I strive to be able to honour my commitments and help others reach their goals and full potential. Helping women who have hit rock bottom and lost their purpose are of utmost importance for me. This is my mission and, if I can assist just one to overcome adversity in her life, find her feet, claim her power and regain her life, I will be successful.

The Path to Success

There is no straight path to success. Perhaps there could be in an ideal world. However, often you get in the way of your own success. It is, to a large degree, dependent on your level of focus and motivation. Which can often be lacking. If you get into the habit of being too 'busy', it is easy to fall prey to distractions that keep you from moving forward. These distractions can be meaningless and unnecessary but, when they are not, they could be just what is needed at that moment. If you are sidetracked and it takes you off course, it could be seen as an excuse to avoid doing what you had set out to accomplish. In which case, you might want to look at why that is. Check in with yourself to make sure you are not procrastinating.

The Full Circle

However, this diversion from your path could be something which is necessary to achieve another goal which may have become more important at this time.

An illustration of this is the time a client of mine was working on her PhD, which she was having quite a bit of difficulty completing. She had some distractions which were keeping her from working on her thesis. After a few sessions with me, she came to the conclusion that, at that time, her PhD was not high on her priority list, although it was still a goal. She had become involved with a project which was higher on her list of values and this is where her passion was at that time. She was fighting with herself about doing what she thought she "should" do rather than what was most important to her at that stage.

Together, I helped her reset her goal of completing her PhD at a later, more realistic time. In the end, she was successful with the project that was "distracting" her and it was extremely successful for her. Within a year, she achieved her PhD and, instead of feeling like a failure and exceedingly tense as she was when she came to me, she was relaxed, happy and celebrating her wins.

As at the time of writing this book, my focus was on this book. I set aside other less important projects to get it completed. By organising my time and splitting up my workload, I could achieve my deadline. Sometimes your path to success may take an alternate route, as you saw with my client. For me, while writing this book the same thing occurred. I surmised that I had initially set an unrealistic time line for writing since this was the first complete book I had tackled. There were times I felt guilty about not doing more, thinking that perhaps this was not a high enough goal for me. I questioned my values around it as well.

I was committed to getting my message out there to help others and that became my driving force. I reset a number of my goals at the time so that success was still in sight. Would staying on course with my original timeline for the book have meant I would have had a straight line to completion? Not necessarily. Life is not that simple because there are usually some bumps or curves in the road that require adjustment and adaptation to enable you to reach your destination. Understanding this can be key when defining success. The circles of reaching a destination may not always be round!

Success is as much about change as it is about learning and growing on the journey. If my mantra "everything happens for a reason" is considered here, the fact that I altered the finalisation of my book meant other opportunities came my way when I had veered off my original path. I do not question myself on why I lost focus but, by doing so, I had other great experiences and recorded certain successes not in my original plan!

If you are to define your success by a single event or level, what happens if you do not reach that level of success again next time? A prime example of this is in the Hollywood film industry. We often hear of actors who follow the road to decline when they get older because they are not the beauty they used to be and are being replaced by younger faces. They lose touch with the reality of who they are now and turn down parts to play a mother or grandmother. They still want to be the 20 something star and struggle to accept that things have changed.

The really successful actors have been those willing to embrace the older roles, and sometimes have become even more successful in the later years of their life. Some examples are Morgan Freeman and Judi Dench. Actresses such as Meryl Streep and Helen Mirren seem to just get better and better. Perhaps it is because they simply love what they do and this defines their success – not a need to be the young film star of their youth. By contrast, other aging stars see themselves as failures now because they are not who they used to be. They have been unable to redefine their perception of success, and sometimes even develop deep emotional problems.

The Full Circle

Andrew Lloyd Webber showcased this tragedy in his hit musical *Sunset Boulevard* where a once famous film star lived in a delusional world of needing to be famous. Other famous people may turn to drugs or alcohol to numb the pain of what they see as rejection or failure. Perhaps they have also fallen into the plastic surgery trap to make themselves look more youthful. They have nothing left in their bag of tricks because they were merely their once off success and nothing else.

One of my clients, an older woman who had many years in the corporate world, was at the stage in her life that she wanted to change course. She wanted to go into her own business yet was feeling like a failure because business was going much slower than anticipated. She had always been extremely successful in her past and queried why she was experiencing difficulty at the time. After a number of sessions where she looked deeply into understanding herself better, she could see that her values were not being met. She reevaluated what her present values were, in view of what she wanted now in life – not what she thought she would be having based on her previous personal and business life. She became less hard on herself and is now running a very profitable consulting business and is happier than she has been for years.

You may have reached a point in your life where you want to change your working life or you have lost your job. You are much older and now, cannot find anything else because of your age. Perhaps you are not needed as much because your children have left home. You may not have the slim waistline and unwrinkled face of days gone by, and your husband has left you for another woman years younger than you. Don't despair – you do have a choice and I am here to help you to learn that none of these reasons are cause for you to give up or fall into the dark abyss. You CAN still have everything. You CAN be happy. Life may be different than it was, but what if it could be better? Isn't that worth working towards?

If success to you is more intangible, you may have a better chance at not crumbling if your situation changes. With a variety of goals to achieve, victory can be more far reaching and diverse. As a result, you would be more centered. If you did not achieve success in one area, you would own it, look at where you did not succeed and change what you need to for the next goal. Failures and setbacks play a significant role in success. Prospering is not just about moving forward and getting things right. Sometimes, you have to get many things wrong before you learn how to get things right. Failure and setbacks will teach us more than success ever can.

"Success is defined just as much by the ability to get back up when you have been knocked down, to keep moving forward when you are weary, and keep believing in your dream when everyone else has walked away."
– Paulette Archer

There are many examples of well-known individuals who have had great success only to lose everything later. Then, before you know it, they are back out there doing something again that gives them triumph once more. They have learnt and are out there doing what it takes, time and time again. They do not let any setback change how they operate in this world; they just get up, brush themselves off and start again.

Some of these people are names we all know: Martha Stewart, Dorothy Hamill, Cyndi Lauper, Kim Basinger, Walt Disney and Richard Branson, to name a few. In my own circle of friends, I have also known people who have lost everything and just started over. They did not give up, so success was theirs once again. Perhaps I even belong in this category.

The Full Circle

> Distinguish whether you have had failures or lessons learnt
> 1. Have you had failures that have taught you about success?
> 2. What have been the lessons you learnt? How have you applied these lessons to your life?

_____

_____

_____

There really are no failures, just opportunities. It is when you look at what has happened and can learn, that you start to grow. Being successful, for me, is about learning from my failures, mistakes or setbacks. I like to think that none of those things really classify as failures, just learning experiences.

If something has not gone according to plan, I look and see why it happened this way and not the way "I planned". Did I lose my motivation? Did I get distracted? Did my life change in the process so this did not mean as much to me as it had? Can I vary something now so I can be successful in this goal? What can I do to change? There is a phrase that leadership author John Maxwell coined called "Failing Forward". He has written a book by the same title. Failure is not failure if you keep moving forward and learn from the experience.

Part of not being held back by defeat is being able to recognise the learning experience and attribute that learning as success. Then take the time to celebrate those wins. They may be small, but they are equally important. We spoke about celebrating successes earlier, and by doing this, you are acknowledging that you have modified something in your life for the better and that you have followed your desired path to transform.

Celebrating will give you a renewed sense of confidence which will then assist you in accomplishing the more difficult and bigger goals you are looking to achieve. It can provide you with the encouragement to continue. It can be a sign that "yes, this goal has been completed" and you put it away to start on something new. Quite often, the small goals are on the pathway to a larger one, so celebrating them gives you the boost to carry on. Acknowledging a success brings the larger goal closer in your sights and to being accomplished.

Self-Perception, Belief, Luck and Success

If we have little belief in ourselves and think we are unsuccessful, it will be harder for us to achieve success. I have had clients who have made comments such as "There's no way I could have done that since I have never done it before", or "I'm not smart, so I couldn't learn that". Limiting beliefs about their age, gender or socioeconomic status can be a catalyst for these types of thoughts. Perhaps they have not had a formal education so do not see themselves capable of earning a good income, for example. Maybe they believe that money only comes to a certain group of highly educated people. Those with poor self-esteem are less likely to set many goals because they fear failure. For them, they believe it is easier not to try than to try and fail.

We already know to be a success, action needs to be taken. If we have limiting beliefs, there is much less probability of that happening. Working on improving your self-esteem and learning to love yourself at this stage is vital. The media carries many stories that appear to be of overnight success. You might look at these stories and think those people are just lucky. Can success happen by accident? If it does, is it really success or just dumb luck? Perhaps some people may believe their success was pure luck. It was about being in the right place at the right time or just knowing the right person. Some people refer to this as having a lucky break. I am not so sure that it has that much to do with luck. If success is based on action or steps taken to accomplish something, having success by accident or dumb luck means that it cannot happen.

Becoming successful means, you have strategies to get you there and with dumb luck, there is nothing. When we hear of success stories, we do not always find out how long it has actually taken the individual to become successful. I would say in the majority of cases, the success came with much hard work, focus and determination. Considering success is different for different people, then let's use an example of success as "winning the lottery".

When you win, you have been successful (of course winning the lottery is just luck). Success could escalate from there if the individual does something useful with the money and manages to keep it and grow it so they are set for life.

Unfortunately, what occurs in many cases when someone is successful because of luck, is that such success can be short lived – especially when winning the lottery. These individuals have not earned the success and, as a result, they spend everything on lavish living. They had not developed good standards around working and looking after their money. They did not have to work for this success, so they have no idea about how to 'work' to keep it. It happens regularly in lotto wins that a few years down the line, people are poorer than before they won. I have known three separate individuals where this is the case – their money gone almost as quickly as it came.

10: Success

> **Success and Opportunities**
> 1. What relationship is there between success and opportunity?
> 2. Do opportunities come to those who seek them out? Why or why not?

_____

_____

_____

Perhaps success has more to do with recognising positive circumstances than being lucky. If you have a specific goal in mind, you position yourself to be on the lookout for opportunities. You know what you want and have a good idea of what will help to achieve it. So, when an opportune moment surfaces, you will not see it as luck but, rather, as a stepping stone to achieving your goal.

Luck insinuates that there was nothing intentional or deliberate in a situation – it is pure chance. Furthermore, when a person is on the lookout for favourable outcomes, it is deliberate and intentional. Successful people are out there looking, seeking results. Opportunities are simply recognising that this may be something that provides a solution.

Successful individuals are constantly looking for better ways of doing things, masterminding to get the best results, testing and evaluating what they have done and even looking for individuals to partner with so their success is heightened. Any opportunity that can possibly fast track this would be considered. This all differs from luck because when you are successful you look at life differently. You look from the positive not the negative and are open and willing to change. Successful people understand the importance of being flexible and are generally interested in newer, better and brighter ways of doing things.

Taking responsibility for your life and being willing to change for better has to do with being flexible. This then, of course, impacts on your performance in life. If you look at life as black and white and are not willing to do what it takes to flourish, then your outcomes may be limited. In order to learn and grow, one must be amenable in both attitudes and actions. We have talked about the fact that high achievers thrive and that it is important to adjust your sails in the quest for goal achievement. This is a sure sign of adaptability. If something is not happening the way you want, it will not be any different unless you change your approach. Flexibility certainly can impact success quite a bit – and for the better.

Now that we have discussed success in some detail, there are six steps I would like to leave you with. These have been instrumental for me in achieving some of my successes. I do believe that they can contribute to your success as well.

STEPS TO SUCCESS

STEP 1	Set goals. Make sure you set the goals using the CREATE framework.
STEP 2	Know your core values so that your goals are in alignment with them.
STEP 3	Take deliberate action to achieve your goals. Create milestones or steps to success.
STEP 4	Have clarity and focus on what you are working on and know why you're working on it.
STEP 5	Be flexible. Be willing to adapt and adjust your plans and strategies to achieve your goals.
STEP 6	Take every experience including setbacks and failures, as an opportunity to learn.

11: Is It Okay To Accept Your Circumstances?

"Acceptance of what has happened is the first step to overcoming the consequences of any misfortune."
– William James

What a powerful thought the word *acceptance* can conjure. However, acceptance has, for many, a very passive connotation in that accepting a situation, person or thing, you are just taking it for what it is. This can be both positive and negative. If the situation was bad or harmful, it is a natural reaction for most people to know something should be done about it. In that case, simple acceptance, thinking that nothing can be done about it, can leave a person without hope. Acceptance is anything but passive. It is not about sitting back, but about taking action and responsibility for my life.

Let's say that you have worked hard and you achieve your goals; then accept the success and celebrate it joyfully and without guilt. Enjoy the fruits of your labour. This is an example of positive acceptance. By the same token, if faced with a difficult situation, you still have a choice. You can accept the things you cannot change or have no control over. You can also accept that you have the power to change what you can – your thoughts, your response, your life. This can bring our circle to completion after working through many steps to get you from where you are to where you want to go.

> **Look at what there is about yourself or your life that you struggle to accept**
>
> 1. What is it? Why do you think you struggle with it?

_____

_____

Acceptance is coming to terms with a situation, even if it was difficult at first to consider. Once I have grasped the idea that this is now my reality, I can accept it, believe it is okay and then take control or responsibility over the things I can change about the situation. Those things may just be my attitude towards it.

I could not change my first husband's mind about having children – I had to accept that. But I was not powerless, I still had a choice. I could have stayed in that marriage with the knowledge that we may never have children. Or, I could choose to leave the relationship with the hope that one day my dream of a family would be fulfilled. This may not ever have eventuated either. However, I felt I would not have been true to myself if I stayed in a childless marriage by choice. I was following my values system, and that is what felt was right for me in those days. I know I made the right decision. As I have shared my story, you know that I chose the latter. It is not to say the decision was easy or my choices were right or wrong. The point is I accepted what I could not change and then took responsibility for the choices I could make.

Acceptance is also about being happy with who I am and how I live my life. Self-acceptance enables me to live a totally different life. Letting go of past issues and learning to accept that they are simply part of my life, has made me happier and more content. Accepting who I am and learning to love myself, despite my faults and mistakes, has given me a freedom I never contemplated.

11: Is It Okay To Accept Your Circumstances?

With acceptance comes responsibility, and I now see things differently when they happen. I see life more from a positive rather than a negative standpoint. I have become more of an optimist in my life, and it is great to feel that way again. I believe I was an optimist in my early life and then, somehow, lost that perspective for a number of years.

> **Examine whether or not you are an optimist, pessimist or realist**
> 1. What is it about you that makes you an optimist, pessimist or realist?
> 2. Has this changed in your life? Do you think it could change again?

_____

_____

_____

_____

Today, I have become more accepting when the hard times come. I am able to look at circumstances differently and my coping mechanisms are better. I can see that the more I fight against something that I do not want, the harder it becomes and the more unsettled I am. On the other hand, if I look more objectively at a situation, I can often see the positives. Then I am satisfied and more peaceful for accepting the situation as it stands. If I have no control over a situation, fighting for what I want but cannot have, is a huge waste of mental and even physical energy. Acceptance is not necessarily easy, but it puts me in a much happier place.

The Full Circle

With acceptance, we are able to grow and develop ourselves. When I got divorced, I thought that the absolute worst had happened to me and I would not be able to go on. However, once I accepted what had happened, it opened many new doors for me. The initial step towards acceptance is the hard part. After that, it gets less difficult. Being able to accept something as it is does not always come easy. It is something I have developed over a rather short period of time in recent years.

If I consciously choose to accept something, I am empowered – it becomes a win–win situation. In other words, irrespective of the outcome, I will be a winner. Acceptance is one of the first steps needed to make change. When we make a decision to change, we are consciously making a choice for our life.

11: Is It Okay To Accept Your Circumstances?

> **Describe how you see acceptance**
> 1. Is acceptance a choice?
> 2. Why is or isn't it a choice?
> 3. How do you think acceptance factors into who you are as a person?
> 4. On a scale of 1-10, how easy (1) or difficult (10) is acceptance for you?
> 5. Do you think that acceptance makes you stronger or weaker as a person?
> 6. What would make acceptance easier for you?

_____
_____
_____
_____
_____
_____
_____

Your world is continually changing and it may not always give you what you want or what you think you want. If life is a continual fight about what lies ahead, there would be little happiness. I can choose to resist or choose to find the positive in the event. I have acquired strategies to get me through the tough times. Sometimes, new situations in my life need to be revisited for me to develop an attitude of acceptance towards them, but it becomes easier and easier the more I learn.

The Full Circle

When I think of the difficult events that have transpired in the last decade or more, I know this is true. Without becoming self-aware or accepting the situation of my divorce, my back issues, nerve damage, decreased mobility and chronic pain, I could be in a totally different state. I don't think of myself as a victim as I have become able to accept these things and flourish instead of withering up and staying in the dark place of the past.

It is essential to understand that acceptance is not about giving in or being passive. It is about taking responsibility and control of your own life. Acceptance is at the core of our personal development and growth as human beings. I have worked with individuals who refused to accept something that would be considered tragic in their lives. They continued to be negative, unforgiving and resentful. They were angry and unhappy and completely fell into the victim mentality. This is not a good place to be and stunts any possibility of personal growth. Assisting them to look at their situation differently and taking steps to change what is not working in their lives is what is needed for growth and change to occur.

At one time, this was me. Somehow, I knew there must be more to life. I found once I had acceptance, everything else in my life changed for the better. The same held true for my clients and can for you as well.

The Hard Part About Acceptance

The hard part about acceptance can be that you have to agree or approve of something that you might otherwise reject. You can question why this has happened and look for reasons, people or things to blame. In that space, you are in denial – which is your defense mechanism. You might talk yourself out of what has happened so you do not hurt as much. Unfortunately, until you accept the truth, you will not make any progress past the hurt. You

11: Is It Okay To Accept Your Circumstances?

might judge what has happened and continually look for answers. All of these things make it harder for you to accept.

My mantra "Everything happens for a reason" has helped me accept certain situations more. Nevertheless, it does not always make it any easier. I may never positively know why something has happened. I just need to trust that it has and that it is for the better. Not everyone agrees with this thought process – there is no right or wrong here. Practicing acceptance can help me live in this world with all of its uncertainties and still feel good about myself and my life. Acceptance can mean that I will go through a certain amount of struggle. However, if I allow my feelings to come up and recognise them for what they are, my acceptance will follow more readily.

Although I may face more challenges and obstacles in my life, I embrace acceptance. Learning more about me and tapping into my values have changed my perspectives and perceptions. With acceptance, I feel as if I have a sense of control. When I think of times when I was unwilling to accede and compare how I feel when I do, the difference is incredible. It is as if there is a 'lightness' in the air. It is as if a weight has been lifted off my shoulders. I feel empowered and motivated.

Some people have the idea that acceptance means you are weak or a pushover. They could not be more wrong. Acceptance makes you stronger in that you have examined the situation with your eyes wide open. You know "this is the way it is" and you have the power to reinterpret how you feel about it, change it if possible, or just leave it. Perhaps the situation has occurred and you cannot change it, but you can change how you view it.

"Acceptance is strength as opposed to weakness."
– Paulette Archer

Is Acceptance Okay or Do You Need to *'Fight Some Battles'?*

With acceptance, you have the choice to decide what you will do. Once again, you cannot change what has happened, only your reality around it can be altered. Acceptance is not about fighting a battle. It is about accepting the truth about a situation. If you come across a condition in your life that is confronting and difficult to accept, you may, at first, deny or reject it and then fall into the victim mode. In this case it is best to have a look at the event for what it is and not as something entirely your fault. Do not make it you. This will put you in the victim mode which prevents you from moving forward.

With acceptance, we move away from becoming a victim. Sometimes you may make a conscious decision about which situations you decide to fight. Quite possibly, if you believe the situation can be reversed, you might consider fighting that battle. However, this needs to be considered carefully.

In my experience with my nerve damage and pain, I did try to fight this battle at the onset. I did not want to accept I had a physical condition which was affected by my activity levels. Instead of listening to my specialists, I wanted to prove they were wrong and that I could do what they said I couldn't. I fought this battle and all it did was disempower me. I was unhappy and got right into the victim mode – denying the fact that I must take it a little easier than before. My denial led to further surgery on my back. I had not accepted and did not do what I was meant to do to keep me well and free from further medical intervention. I was fighting a lost battle by not accepting.

Throughout my life, I had been used to a certain level of activity and physical fitness – core values for me – and I did not accept that this had changed.

11: Is It Okay To Accept Your Circumstances?

> **Look at acceptance and your life**
> 1. Have you ever made a conscious choice about which battles to fight?
> 2. How can acceptance empower you?
> 3. Have you ever recognised that your failure to accept was actually putting you into victim mode? If so, what did you do to change it?
> 4. How will acceptance benefit you?

_____
_____
_____
_____
_____
_____
_____

Now that I have truly accepted my situation, I have adjusted my activity levels within the range I can tolerate. I gradually work up to more and, perhaps, over time I will be able to do even more – I just do not rush it. I still have the pain and discomfort; nothing has changed except my attitude toward it. Because I have accepted my pain, I believe I have less. Denial made the pain worse.

I persist with my exercises, stretches and whatever is needed to feel my best. When I have a bad day, I take it for what it is. I rest, meditate and do light exercise to recharge me for later. I no longer refute my inability to be as physical as I once was. I look at it from a positive rather than negative standpoint. I consider other activities and am grateful for what I do have and not resentful and angry for what I don't have.

By accepting, it does not mean I have given up. Since I am not fighting the situation, I am not wasting energy on circumstances that, for the most part, are beyond my control. I can keep up with regular positive exercise that will help with my mobility and pain levels, such as Yoga, Pilates and walking daily. I can swim or participate in aqua aerobics. I also avoid those things that I know aggravate my situation. I slowly increase the activities I engage in so that I do not have a relapse and I can keep tabs on what works and what does not.

I rest when I need to and make sure I avoid what is referred to as the *boom and bust* of chronic pain. This means that I look at my daily activities and when I feel great, I avoid overdoing it, which is the tendency in chronic pain. If I overdo it when I feel good (the boom), then what can and usually does happen is that I will fall flat on my face for the next few days because I have over done it (the bust). This has been hard for me to do and the same holds true for many people in similar situations. I can acknowledge that I have accepted my condition here because I have been successful at keeping the extreme pain at bay and avoiding the boom/bust circle most of the time.

> *"Acceptance allows you to make a choice about your life. If you choose to accept something which may be difficult in the beginning, ultimately it will lead to your happiness. Fighting the same thing will lead to wasted energy and unhappiness."*
> **– Paulette Archer**

We have talked about change and know that change is inevitable in the world we live in. Acceptance allows you to live here with

11: Is It Okay To Accept Your Circumstances?

fewer struggles and more control. When attached to self, (self-acceptance), acceptance shows that you are happy within; you love and are comfortable with who you are right now and how you are living your life. That may change, of course, but for this moment in time you have acceptance.

We may not like what has happened, but we can choose to accept things for what they are. This ties in so well with my thoughts and feelings about my mantra "everything happens for a reason". Perhaps it is because I am able to "accept", that this has so much value for me. I may not know why. I can look to see what the reason may be for something happening; however, I can accept the situation without ever knowing. So, for you, how do you feel about acceptance and everything happening for a reason? Do you think acceptance would be easier for you? Let's take a look.

12: Everything Happens For A Reason

"Success is not final, failure is not fatal: it is the courage to continue that counts."
– Winston Churchill

This phrase, "Everything happens for a reason", has become somewhat of a personal mantra in recent years. In writing this Chapter, I contemplated how this came to be. It has to some degree always been part of my thinking, even as a child. Perhaps it was because my mother regularly told me this, when I questioned why we had to move or why something had been unpredictable in its outcome.

Later in life, this phrase resurfaced when times were hard. I do not want to go into a religious tangent here; however, I believe in the almighty plan. This along with my mother's influence and my Catholic upbringing may have shaped these thoughts. I would not say I was consciously aware of this thought; I believe it lay dormant in my unconscious mind and would reappear from time to time.

The Full Circle

> Everything happens for a reason
> 1. Is this true for you?
> 2. Express why or why not.

_____

_____

_____

_____

This phrase is one that has helped me tremendously in getting over the most unpleasant events that materialise in life – not just for me, but for many people worldwide. Even now when I see the news and hear of a particularly hateful or tragic state of affairs, I think about this phrase. It brings me to question what the purpose is for something like that to occur. Even if I do not find clear answers, it helps me come to terms with those situations.

If it is something that affects me in a personal way, I know some how it will be significant in my life – especially if I learn from it. There are many thoughts around this as well, and "everything happens for a reason" can mean more than being supernatural or divine. I look at it from the point, that we cannot always know why events transpire as they do. It probably does not even matter. However, if there is something difficult you are dealing with; by looking for a lesson, I believe it can empower you to look for the good in a situation so that the negative is easier to accept.

12: Everything Happens For A Reason

> Discuss how important is it for you to know the reason why a situation has occurred
>
> 1. Do you think it is always possible to discover it?
> 2. How much time do you think you should spend searching for the answer? Is it that important?
> 3. Could you move on from an event even if an explanation never really becomes clear?
> 4. Are you aware of any unknowns that you think might be holding you back?
> 5. If the reason is not what you expected, would you be able to accept it?

_____
_____
_____
_____
_____
_____
_____
_____

An explanation is important for me personally, despite the fact that it does not always become apparent. Since I do not want to be obsessing over getting answers, quite often, if the reason does not surface fairly quickly, I choose to just leave it and move on. Why something may have resulted could become evident much later and sometimes the reason may never be forthcoming. Whatever the case, I trust it has happened for the better. Wasting time and physical or emotional energy on something you have no control over can lead to a state of depression or worse- acting aggressively toward others when something has not gone the way you would have liked.

When something ensues that tests you — an event that is not what you would have liked to occur — you can take strength from it. You have the ability to think about what has happened and consciously draw from the experience and grow from it. Often you hear about situations where, through adversity, an individual rose to greater heights. Having a challenging event occur only gave the person more reason to forge ahead and do well. Is it possible that the reason this has happened to one individual, is to teach many a lesson?

How many times do we hear inspirational stories from people who have been affected by some tragedy or disaster? When I hear of these things and how a person has risen from them to achieve greatness, I am truly inspired and moved — hopefully to do more myself. Stories are common with just these sorts of crises.

Someone whose child is abducted and perhaps murdered can be an advocate for 'stranger danger', for instance, so that more children and parents can become aware of dangerous situations. Cases of domestic violence happen way too regularly — whether it is physical, mental, or sexual abuse to children or adults, to spouses, family members or the general public. Those affected can also become advocates, which can make huge headway in changing legislation to help those individuals. We saw this happening with my friend who had the autistic son. Examples like this reinforce my belief that everything happens for a reason — if we get the learning, we become empowered.

Perhaps an individual has a family member who has survived cancer, a stroke or a sudden heart attack. They, in turn, spread

12: Everything Happens For A Reason

the word regarding self-checks, self-care and life changes, which inspires others to be more proactive in terms of looking after their own health. This, ultimately, can lead to the prevention of further unnecessary deaths.

A previous client of mine suffered a heart attack at an early age (45). This person was quite healthy, however, was under quite a bit of mental pressure due to her business worries. Of course, it was a total shock to her, as well as her entire family and there was disbelief that it could be happening to someone who was, for all intents and purposes, fit and well, with no evidence of any prior heart disease in her, or her family. The thought that everything happens for a reason here became evident to me, and fortunately to her.

This was a major wakeup call with regard to her anxiety levels which were certainly the cause of the heart attack. I have had friends to which similar health issues occurred and all warning signs were ignored. My client however, made the decision to sell her business and take steps to further reduce her stress. As far as she was concerned, her heart attack was a warning that her life was at risk. She could do something about it or suffer the consequences, which next time may have been fatal. She loved what she had been doing. However, she recognised that she was exceptionally tense due to financial constraints. From that point on, she settled into a very low stress job rather than running her own business which was a constant worry. She never had any more trouble with her heart and became strong and fit once again.

When something goes wrong, many of you would like to give up and shut down. I had done the same at times. Yet, if I become bitter and resentful, it can lead to anger or behaviour which is self-destructive. This is seen all too often in cases of domestic violence. Acting out gets you nowhere. The incident has occurred and that part cannot be altered.

The Full Circle

Media highlights circumstances where an individual will harm innocent people because of the anger they foster after what they consider was an injustice done to them, at some point in their life. But this is harmful. The situation has occurred. Some of these situations may be extreme and, for all the energy and emotion wasted acting out on people who have nothing to do with it, is counterproductive. Unfortunately, it can be difficult for some individuals to stop and think and learn from their past. They have been deeply scarred and it takes time and effort to work through these things. These people need a lot of help, and this is a case that is more extreme than what we are looking at here.

Life is about your experiences and how you are shaped from them, regardless of whether they are good or bad experiences. You act in accordance with your outlook on life and the values attached to it. There are those of us who develop and others who do not. You can use adversity to become better and stronger individuals, who are capable of greatness. It is a choice.

> **If you acknowledge 'the reason' is the learning experience**
> 1. Does this happen often or just for certain events?
> 2. When you hear the phrase "everything happens for a reason", what do you think or feel?
> 3. Why do you think you feel this way?

_____

_____

_____

_____

Words of Comfort, Words of Caution

While this phrase 'it happens for a reason' has been a great comfort for me, others think of it merely as an empty platitude. You will see it the way you choose. There is no right or wrong. Communication is important and if you use this phrase, when speaking to someone who may have just suffered devastating news, it could be seen as an empty platitude. Being empathetic is about being in someone else's shoes and, if we do not know what to say in times of dreadful news, it may just be better to be silent.

Being silent is more helpful if appropriate words do not surface. You need to be cautious that what you say does not come across as meaningless or inappropriate. Support those who need it by staying with them, be silent and listen. Be the shoulder they need at this time. Think of ways in which you can support the person who is hurting by doing something for the individual instead. Help them with their errands, housework, grocery shopping or meals – anything that will ease the burden on them. You may not know how they feel, but they will be able to experience your support in a very real way.

Empower Yourself

The phrase "everything happens for a reason" can be empowering because all of your experiences in life contribute to you becoming the person you are. It is good to grow from positive experiences, but sometimes the most significant growth comes from the trying times. Being able to smile in the face of adversity is a sure sign that you are moving forward in a positive direction. With that perspective on life, you can become more balanced. You can learn from everyone you meet – family, friends, teachers, peers, lovers or even adversaries. There will always be something you can take away. The next similar experience for you could then be handled in a more desirable way.

The Full Circle

Oftentimes, you will take things in unconsciously. It is through interaction with others that you form your own thoughts and opinions. If you can look deeper into situations that may be more difficult for you, you can learn better coping mechanisms for the future. I have mentioned when this phrase became very significant for me and became words I live by. Although the worst aspects of that time (when my husband left) were yet to come, believing there was a reason for the marriage split up helped me through. When I finally accepted, it was for the best. I could see that even though the experience was overwhelming, it was the beginning of something new in my life. Change was forced on me, and in the process, I started to rediscover who I was and what I wanted out of life.

This new life would never have been possible if the separation had not occurred. I have grown so much since then that I am eternally grateful for that fateful day. I soon appreciated that change was possible so I could become a better person for myself, my children and everyone in my life.

While coaching a woman trying to become pregnant a couple of years ago, she obsessed about why she could not conceive and how unfair it all was. We covered a fair bit of ground regarding her belief system and values. Over time, she came to understand that, in fact, there was a very good reason why pregnancy never occurred for her. As it turned out, she had an opportunity to adopt her foster children, something she might not have considered if the case was different. It turned out that, for her, this became very meaningful and she no longer worried or was concerned that she was unable to conceive.

There is a multitude of resources these days to assist you in becoming the best you can be. The unfortunate thing is that many people still do not imagine or know that help is so close. Change is possible for everyone to have the life they desire. You can choose

12: Everything Happens For A Reason

the life you desire as long as you are open and willing to learn from yours, as well as other people's experiences – whether you believe they happen for a reason or not.

You cannot control everything that happens, only your reactions to them. Those that you have no control over can be learning experiences which may take you to a better path – which was the case for me. It is not necessary for you to be the same as everyone else. You can be an individual. You can strive for your best outcome. You do not need to become a puppet to other people or circumstances. You can have control and life can be good, even when it is challenging! You can choose the life you desire!

Conclusion: The Full Circle

"Develop success from failures. Discouragement and failure are two of the surest stepping stones to success."
– Dale Carnegie

I sometimes wonder: "Will we ever truly get to that place where everything is good"? I do not know the answer to that question. Perhaps you will and perhaps you won't. Even so, ultimately, it is up to you. I would like to believe we can get there. It depends on who you are and what it is that you want from life. Your potential as a human being is limitless. But I do know that unless you make changes in your life, unless you start to look for opportunities, then more than likely, you will not find that place of contentment.

Because life is a journey, there is the opportunity to continually become more informed, thereby, transforming your life. If you embrace this, you will always be reaching new heights. As you move through each stage of the circle of your life, you will be different if for no other reason, but that you have aged and have changed in the process.

The Full Circle

> **Give thought to the next step in *your* journey**
> Write down a few items of importance for you concentrate on.

_____

_____

_____

_____

Some people do not change much because they choose to stay in their comfort zones. They have little desire for anything different in their lives. They do not yearn for more and, most often, do not even consider that there is more out there. If that is the case, will their circle be complete?

Change for me is more unconscious. I am not always actively looking for more or not happy with what I have, but my awareness is greater. I find more desirable events occur because I am happier in my life. I take steps on a regular basis to improve my life for the better, whether physically or emotionally. Therefore, the way I handle life is on a higher level than before. I look for new challenges to keep my mind active and my life interesting. Since life is a journey, I believe it is about the path I take and what happens on that journey as opposed to where I end up. Getting to the destination is half the fun! Everything and everyone that comes into my life influences it to some degree. Those experiences help shape me.

Many individuals are searching for something more, wanting something better in their life. This can be the case if you are not happy with your life. Is there any self-love? Have you become complacent and not doing anything to change your current situation? Are you living at effect and blaming others for your unhappiness? You most likely will stay just that way, doing the same things over and over again, making the same mistakes and having difficulty finding happiness or that place where everything is wonderful, positive and satisfying. This is why contentment and happiness in life is ultimately up to you. I have come across many people in my life who spend way too much time complaining about what they do not have yet doing nothing about changing anything in their lives.

Appreciating the Journey

Going through life with your eyes wide open and being accepting to what may come your way, is one way to appreciate the journey more. Another is being curious about life and what it has to offer. Ask questions of yourself and others in an effort to learn. Don't just take what someone says or does as the only way or solution. Consider that there may be more than one way to do something. Experiment a little or a lot. Be willing to think outside the box. Get out of your comfort zone and enjoy life with all it has to offer. Be positive in your outlook and take responsibility for your life – don't leave it up to someone else. Be confident and trust your decisions. Be your own unique self and be willing to change. Learn to love asking questions. Be conscious of reaching your full potential. Do not waste your time on the negatives.

It is easy for us to follow a leader; however, being the leader and being in command takes a lot more skill. Find your own path to follow, even if it is against the norm. Choosing to live your life on your terms and according to your dreams can lead to an extraordinary appreciation of life and what it has to offer. If there is something you truly believe in, take a stand on it. Don't just say you are not happy with the way something is going, remedy it! Be proactive in order to avoid an outcome that you are dissatisfied with; make the effort to change the situations that are necessary for you to live with integrity and within your values.

The Full Circle

> **Appraise what you appreciate most about your life**
> 1. Are you on track to reaching your full potential or do you still have a long way to go?
> 2. Have you found your own path?
> 3. Do you live life on your own terms? Do you want to?
> 4. Do you believe it is worth it or are you willing to stay where you are because it is what you know and is 'comfortable'?

_____
_____
_____
_____
_____

Learn to become the entrepreneur of your life. True entrepreneurs are excellent at making decisions as to how they want to run their lives for their benefit and for the benefit of others. They look at making the world a better place and think up new ways to do so. They build up teams to assist them, with the intention of creating value and enriching lives. An entrepreneur will see opportunities when others do not. You do not need to be a business owner to think like an entrepreneur. You can apply these principles to your personal life even if you are in a salaried job or even unemployed. Developing the mindset of an entrepreneur can lead to greater growth and appreciating your journey more.

Conclusion: The Full Circle

"You are never too old to learn and grow or be ambitious. It really doesn't matter what stage of life you are in, if you are willing, there are always opportunities to learn."
– Paulette Archer

When I consider all of the changes that have occurred in my life, just in terms of my physical environment, if I had not adapted, where would I be? I might still be using a typewriter instead of a computer. If I insisted on writing letters to my friends instead of calling on the phone, I might not have much of a social life. If I wasn't accepting of my circumstances around my divorces I may still be wallowing in a pit of despair.

I like to look upon my father as an example. He retired from work at age 59 but did not spend much time sitting back. Instead, he spent the next 30 plus years involved in volunteer work with various organisations. Only after he turned 90 and got tired easily, did he eventually take proper retirement. Through his volunteer work, he was always learning. It stretched him mentally and he never developed an elderly mindset.

He started using a computer for the first time in his 70's. In his 80's, he commenced online banking and bought a mobile phone. He also learnt to cook. Part of this was out of necessity, as my mother passed away and she had always done the cooking. This, in itself, was a huge 'get out of your comfort zone', since he never did the cooking or housework beforehand. Even when my mother passed away, he did not expect others to look after him the way she had. Instead, he went about learning how to do all the household chores needed for him to look after himself. He had a wonderful life in retirement with my mother and, even though he did his volunteer work, he still had time to play plenty of golf and socialise with friends – plus my parents travelled where and when they wanted to.

The Full Circle

> Learning and growing
> 1. When do you think you will stop learning?
> 2. Do you still have room to learn and grow?
> 3. Is there anything in your life that is stopping you from starting to learn and grow?

_____

_____

_____

_____

_____

This may seem a bit simplistic; however, it is an example of how we can always make change if we are willing. Change is not age-disaggregated. Start from right where you are. I have often heard of individuals who have set out to earn a university degree well into their 70's or 80's. I know a woman who started her own business well into her 70's and another who obtained a university degree at 80. In my life, some of the biggest changes and learning experiences happened after I turned 50. I continue with my study of personal development. Part of this is looking at ways to improve and change the way I run my life. The only thing stopping someone from learning and growing is their self!

What is it that you think you cannot do because of your situation? Where do you need help? Is it to feel better about yourself, adjust to unexpected changes in your life due to a death, separation, divorce, health or wealth reasons? Are you looking for your purpose? Have you hit rock bottom and desire to become alive and thrive once again? Whatever the case, there is hope and help available for you to overcome any adversity in your life, in order to thrive. It is time for you to find your feet, claim your power and regain your life!

The FAB MAP

When I started my coaching business, it was called FAB MAP Coaching. This was an acronym for Focus, Action, Balance, Motivation, Achievement and Personal growth. Focus, action, balance and motivation are very important in personal development. If practiced, they lead to achievement and continued personal growth.

Nothing will change for you if no action is taken. Having the desire for something to be different in our lives will only become a reality if we make the decision to change and take the steps needed for this to occur. The steps that we take are a journey and we can MAP this out for ourselves by goal setting. FAB, is also a shortened version of the word fabulous. I want to have a fabulous life and I can see that happening, if I set a journey following my MAP for change.

The FAB MAP is also a wonderful metaphor for my life. If I was to set out in my car to travel to a different state, for instance, I might never reach my destination if I have no clear idea of the way I need to go. I see life as being no different. If I was to set out on my journey of life, without a map to head me in the right direction, I may just move around aimlessly not making any progress. I may change course from time to time, to travel into areas that I may not have considered. I might get off the highway to explore the surrounding towns; however, my goal for reaching a certain destination will continue to be there, so it will be possible for me to get to where I want to go. As I set out on my travels, I journey there and back completing a circle – just as I do in my life.

At different times in my life I have set out to 'travel' to one area and actually have never reached it. This too is okay if I have mapped out the new direction I want to take. My wish is for all of you reading this book to be able to MAP out your lives so that you can reach your FAB life and full potential – not move around aimlessly in your journey. If I can help with this, then I am successful in my quest.

Learning from The Journey

How can you ensure that past experiences remain positive influences on your journey, even if they were negative occurrences? Each episode in life could have some learning attached to it. You need to make the choice as to how it will impact your being. You can choose to be at cause and take responsibility and look for the positive in each event – especially if it was a negative one to start with. A wonderful quote by **Eckhart Tolle** sums it up perfectly: *"Whatever the present moment contains, accept it as if you had chosen it. Always work with it, not against it."*

Conclusion: The Full Circle

> **Your journey**
>
> 1. If you were to draw up a FAB MAP for your life, how would you do in each area?
> 2. What can you learn from your journey so far?
> 3. Do you live in the moment, the past or the future?
> 4. In your journey to date, have you been living with responsibility or blame?
> 5. What has been the value of your experiences until now?
> 6. What do you think the next part of your journey will hold for you?

_____

_____

_____

_____

_____

_____

_____

If you fight what has happened to you in life, you will be less happy, looking for blame and reasons that may never be evident. In this case, you are more likely to be living at effect and your journey will be rough. For each of your life's experiences, you have a choice as to how to deal with them.

Since life is a journey, it will be filled with many occurrences – some good and some bad. Just like the car trip to a new state. You may encounter rough roads, bad weather, and you may even have a flat tire or engine trouble. Your journey may be slower than expected, have more traffic or you may get lost. Not all of these things will be pleasant, but you can still learn from them. You can make better plans next time, have the car checked before setting off, know how much time is needed and allow for the unknown or unexpected so that you can eventually make it to your destination. This is a perfect analogy for goal setting. In life, that is your purpose – to attain or reach your goal, whether conscious or not.

Your challenges will make you stronger if you let them. They are inevitable and, if viewed as blessings, you will get way more out of life. This is one choice you make. Make the most out of the situation and learn from it. Or you can focus on all the negatives and let your life just pass you by since you are dwelling on what if's and why me's. By focusing on the negative, you will certainly miss many chances life has to offer. Remember, you cannot change the past – only your perception of it and your mind moving forward.

Keeping myself uplifted and motivated towards a positive life is necessary in order to stay on track. It is easy to regress and live at effect. That is okay from time to time, as long as I pick myself up and not allow it to continue. In the next part of my journey, taking responsibility for my life will ensure that I continue in the direction in which I am heading right now. Understanding myself and what I want from my life will keep me on track. My goal is to continue to keep myself motivated and confident, and mixing with like-minded positive people. In this way, there will be no need to "blame others" for anything that is not working in my life.

If I strive to reach my full potential and look at what I have created so far, then I will be less likely to have doubts about myself and my abilities. Self-love, in itself, will prevent the feelings of doubt coming in. I will be more likely to identify all that I have achieved in the past and how this has shaped my life. If I have more self-love,

Conclusion: The Full Circle

it will mean that I am less likely to be influenced by others in a negative way. In the past, I often worried about what others said or thought about me. As long as I am not influenced by this into the future, then I am more likely to achieve my goals and be successful in life.

Being self-assured is very important, just as is keeping away thoughts of self-doubt. If I keep at cause as much as possible, then the next circle of my journey will be easier than the last. These days, I am more focused on what I want. I am setting better and more realistic goals and actually executing them. As a result, I have a more favourable outlook than ever before. Living for myself and my goals is making my life more meaningful; yet, I can still do for others and in time make a difference in this world.

Taking responsibility and keeping positive as much as possible is important if I am to maintain my happy, contented state of mind. This has a huge part to play in my ongoing journey. It is interesting how differently I look at life now compared to earlier times. I do not always get it right. On the other hand, I stop and think more often than I did previously. Now I make better decisions and believe I come up with better solutions. There is much that I do differently now compared to my past. I am guided by me – living my life – instead of doing what someone else wants me to do to benefit their life.

I make my own decisions and take time out for me. I celebrate my wins and I look at what I want and plan for those things. I have always been fairly disciplined in my life. However, now I set myself goals on a daily, weekly, monthly and yearly basis. I am also open to changes in my course, if I see fit, without guilt. If I am faced with a challenge or obstacle to overcome, I may have a bit of an inward complaint to start with, but then find that it can become insignificant in the end. I evaluate before reacting. I do not bother other people with those little "niggling" thoughts, and so they are not blown out of proportion or take over my life. They come and then they go.

Of particular importance is to ensure I have plenty of time for reading. Many of the books I choose are focused on the area of personal development which keeps me feeling positive. I also endeavour to keep a gratitude journal. This is included in my daily activities so that I am constantly reminded that I have much for which to be thankful. I look at what I can do to extend myself and move out of my comfort zone. This keeps me feeling more alive and becomes a positive motivator for me. I can look at those things and feel a sense of accomplishment and success in my life. Volunteering and being able to help others less fortunate remains important.

What is My Life Journey So Far? What Could Yours Be Like into The Future?

Living at cause means I make decisions for my life with purpose. If there is something that I believe will benefit me or those around me, I can make the decision to have this and not worry about what someone else may say about it. I no longer look at what others are doing because it is not about "others" but, rather, about me and my life. What they think only affects them, not me. I consider the consequences of my actions on others, although I do not take responsibility for the way they react to situations or how they feel – as in the past. This alleviates stress that I would have previously caused myself. Nowadays, I am less likely to react to the whims or emotional states of others.

Conclusion: The Full Circle

> **Ponder these questions**
> 1. What does taking responsibility, acceptance and empathy have to do with your journey?
> 2. How can living at cause change your journey into the future?

_____

_____

_____

_____

Some years back I never would have imagined that this would be my life in my 60's. It is a life that is full and happy. I can reminisce and be grateful for all the experiences I have had thus far. These experiences are particularly valuable in my coaching business. Having the ability to help others realise their own potential, find their feet and start taking charge of their life is my goal. Nothing on my journey of life need ever be wasted. The journey continues and I, for one, am enjoying the ride!

More Circles – The End Is the Beginning

When I set out to write this book, it was partly to share how I was able to start to take control of my life after some pretty low times. I wanted to reach out to women who had lost their purpose and may feel that they have no choice but to stay where they are. I wanted to share with them that there is a way to find happiness again.

My life has not been overly dramatic, even though, at times, it has been painful. I do not feel I have extraordinary skills or abilities. My life is quite normal, yet, it has taught me so much. In fact, some of the toughest times have taught me the most. I love myself and have let go of self-doubt. I accept circumstances for what they are and take responsibility for my own actions and choices. I can let go of regrets and appreciate that everything happens for a reason. Sometimes that reason becomes apparent in time and sometimes I never know why. But I have learnt to move on, regardless, without regrets, and gain more understanding from each experience.

> *"Accept responsibility for your life. Know that it is you who will get you where you want to go, no one else."*
> **– Les Brown**

I acknowledge that this was not always the case. There were times in my life that I blamed everyone and everything else for my unhappiness. I wanted change but felt powerless to affect it. I thought that other people in my life had to change. I expected that if my circumstances were different, I might be happy. I did not know then that the key to my happiness was in my own hands all that time. Change was up to me. I did not need to take responsibility and bear the burden of blame for everything that was making me so dispirited. I had to only take responsibility for *my* actions and choices. More importantly, I had to accept that I could not control everything in life or expect change from others.

An amazing thing happened when I really started to understand the difference between living at effect and living at cause – I started to discover strengths and abilities I did not know I had. I started to find peace and contentment I had not felt in a long time. Most of all, I started to feel that I was finally in control of my life. This journey – this full circle – has been an experience worth living.

Now I can step out of my comfort zone, even when it means facing my fears. One of these life changing experiences was learning to swim and to scuba dive. What an experience that was.

Conclusion: The Full Circle

When I look at that experience, I see it as a metaphor for my life. The circles of my life most certainly have been repeated. From the very beginning, I needed to comprehend what I needed to function effectively and greatly in life. The floundering I did a good part of my adult life was much like learning to swim. I was afraid of so much in my life – I was afraid of the "deep water" and I fought going into the deep end for so long. It was not until I got into the "deep end" that I was able to realise I could, in fact, function effectively on my own and swim to the finish line.

I did not need anyone to hold my hand and take me there – I could do it myself. As a child, I also had to learn to move and adjust to new environments and feel comfortable in those new waters each time the family relocated. I had my parents' support for the first 16 years, and always felt I could call on them if need be, although I wanted to learn to do for myself. I lost that in the middle years when I wanted to be loved and protected by outside forces.

Until I "figured out" how to love and care for myself, the circles of despair kept rolling around with no change. But then, I finally "learnt to swim" and go into the very deepest end when I began to scuba dive. I found something wonderful there. I discovered I was worth loving for myself, not for anyone else, and I could and would be able to live on my own even when I had to face obstacles. There may have been sharks or other barriers to avoid, but I "finally got it" and conquered! Through all of this, I have found out how empowering and inspiring experiences that I have had throughout my life can be. It is worth stepping outside of your comfort zone – even when it is intimidating. It makes you feel like you are on top of the world when you have conquered a fear.

Inspiration can come from anywhere, and you do not need to be a rock star to inspire people. I have met so many individuals who have inspired me simply by taking on challenges or persevering through difficult circumstances.

The Full Circle

I can see even though I am now in my 60's, that my journey of discovery and growth is far from over. Every experience can teach me something if I am open to it. I am far from perfect. Sometimes I do lapse into living at effect. I feel sorry for myself and fall into victim mode. The difference now is I do not dwell there.

My life is like an onion. (Another circle). As I peel back one layer, another layer is exposed. I can always gain knowledge. As long as I continue to do so, I will continue developing. I have found happiness and success in unexpected places. I am content and for now, I have come a few full circles. There will undoubtedly be many more. I look forward to all that life has in store.

If you are stuck in that place where you feel you have no control, I want to let you know you do not have to stay there. You can take back control of your life. You can stop being the victim and find the happiness and contentment you long for. I know this because I have been there and know what it feels like. I also know how wonderful it feels to take responsibility for my life and be in control once again. It will be challenging, but as the saying goes "I'm not saying it will be easy, I'm saying it will be worth it!"

"You have one life. Let it be the best life you can have. Learn to live at cause and have no regrets. You will be surprised at how much you can learn to love life and love yourself. Embrace stepping out of your comfort zone because that is where the magic happens!
Find your feet, claim your power and regain your life now!"
– Paulette Archer

RESOURCES

The Full Circle

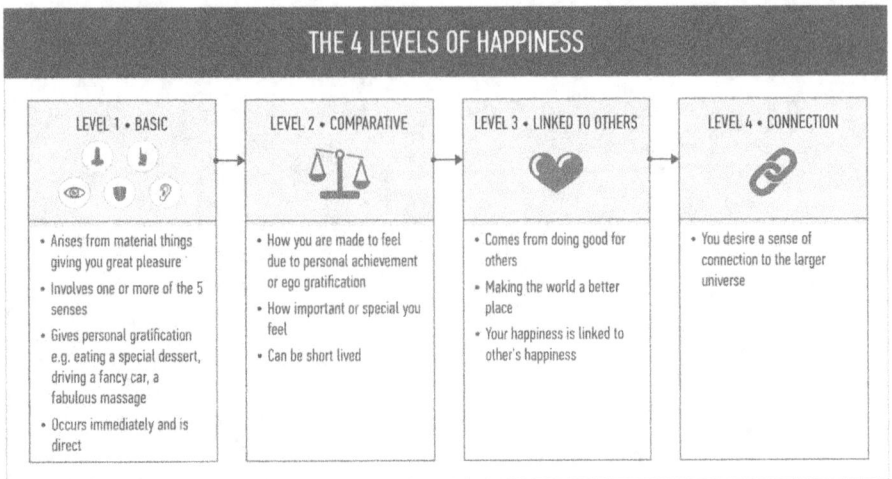

STEPS TO WRITING AN AFFIRMATION

STEP 1 — Consider your goals before writing an affirmation. Make sure this relates to what you want and how you normally behave.

STEP 2 — Make sure you write it down in a positive way. Your affirmation should be what you want not what you don't want.

STEP 3 — Simplicity is best so that you are able to remember the affirmation.

STEP 4 — The affirmation needs to be in the present tense as if it is already part of you.

STEP 5 — The more emotion the better. When you say your affirmation get excited and really feel it.

STEP 6 — Affirmations work best when they are repeated regularly and as often as possible during the day. When you wake up, throughout the day and before going to sleep. You can have them written down in various places so you will constantly be reminded about them or record them so you can replay it back to yourself.

The Full Circle

STEPS TO SUCCESS

STEP 1	Set goals. Make sure you set the goals using the CREATE framework.
STEP 2	Know your core values so that your goals are in alignment with them.
STEP 3	Take deliberate action to achieve your goals. Create milestones or steps to success.
STEP 4	Have clarity and focus on what you are working on and know why you're working on it.
STEP 5	Be flexible. Be willing to adapt and adjust your plans and strategies to achieve your goals.
STEP 6	Take every experience including setbacks and failures, as an opportunity to learn.

Resources

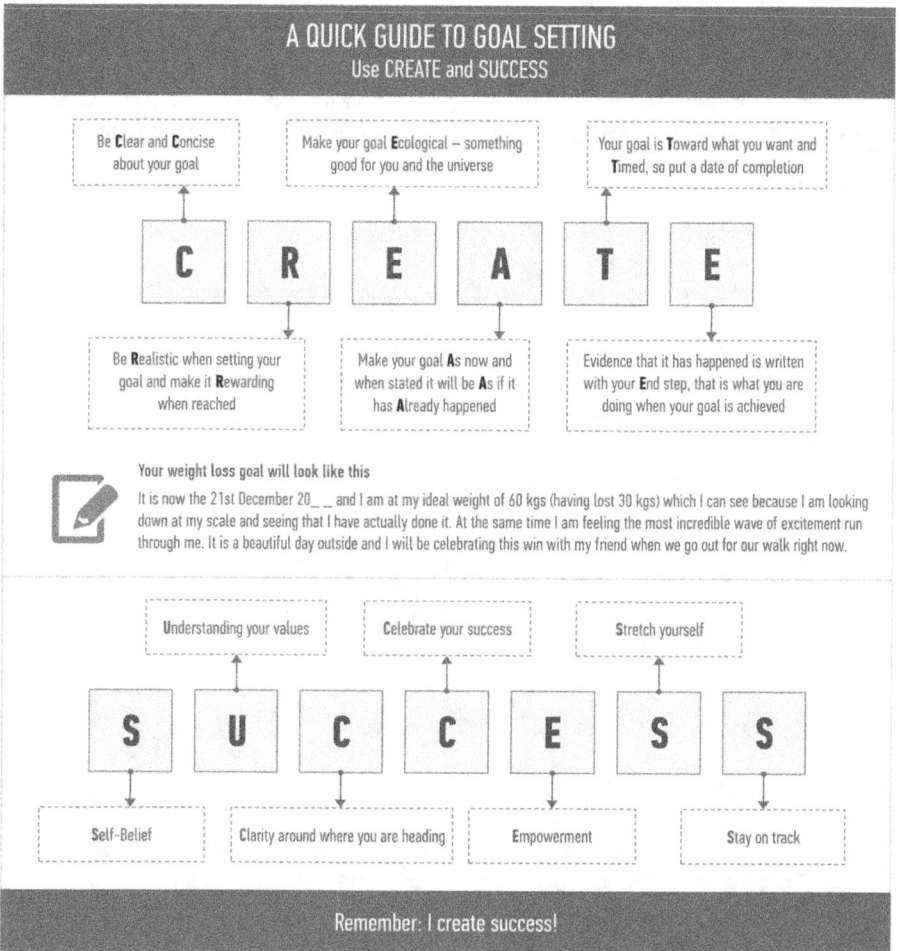

The Full Circle

Your Lifestyle Circle

This is a simple exercise for you to evaluate yourself in 10-12 different areas of your life. Create a *Lifestyle Circle* as demonstrated in the diagram:

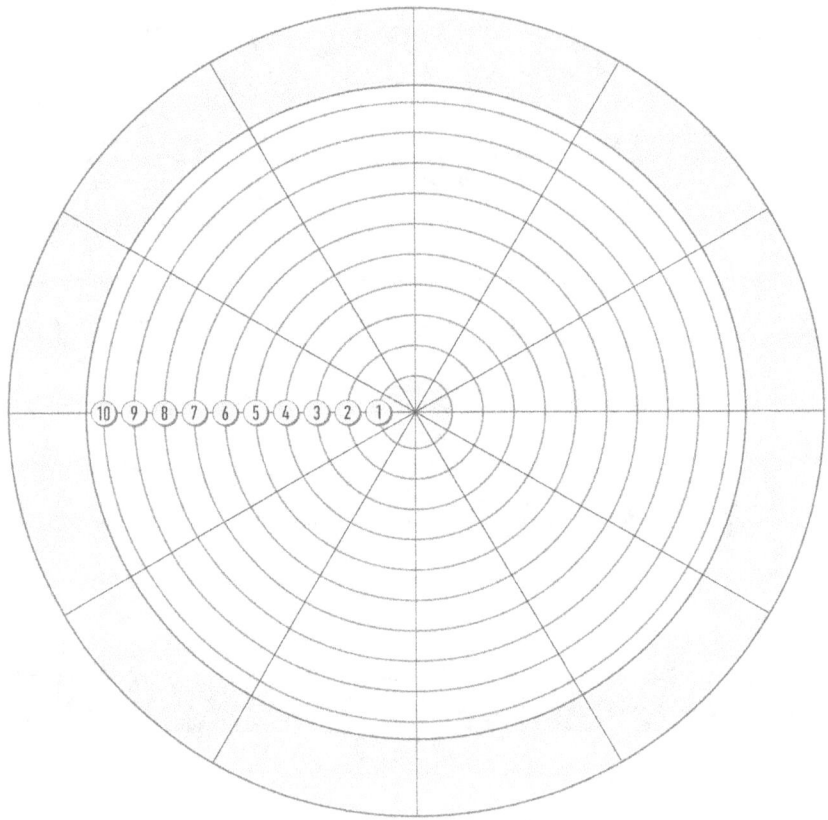

You can select labels from the list below or create your own.

Label each section of the circle with a different area of your life. This circle will represent the balance in your life. If you want to get more detailed, you can subdivide a section. For instance: for Health you could have Physical or Mental Health; Finances could be Cash Flow, Savings and/or Investments, etc.

Resources

List of Possible Section Labels:

- Time Management, Use of Time
- Health – Physical and/or Mental, Physical Fitness
- Personal and/or Professional Growth and/or Development
- Finances – Wealth, Money, Cash Flow, Savings, Investments
- Giving, Donation of Time and/or Money, Philanthropic Efforts
- Career, Work, Job, Self-Employment, Business Owner, Entrepreneur
- Communication – Personal and/or Professional
- Relationships, Personal, Family, Social, Romantic, Friendships, Significant Others
- Stress Management
- Physical Environment, Home and/or Workplace
- Spiritual Development
- Recreation, Fun
- Self Confidence, Self Esteem

The Full Circle

See the example of how your *Lifestyle Circle* may look with 12 possible areas of your life listed:

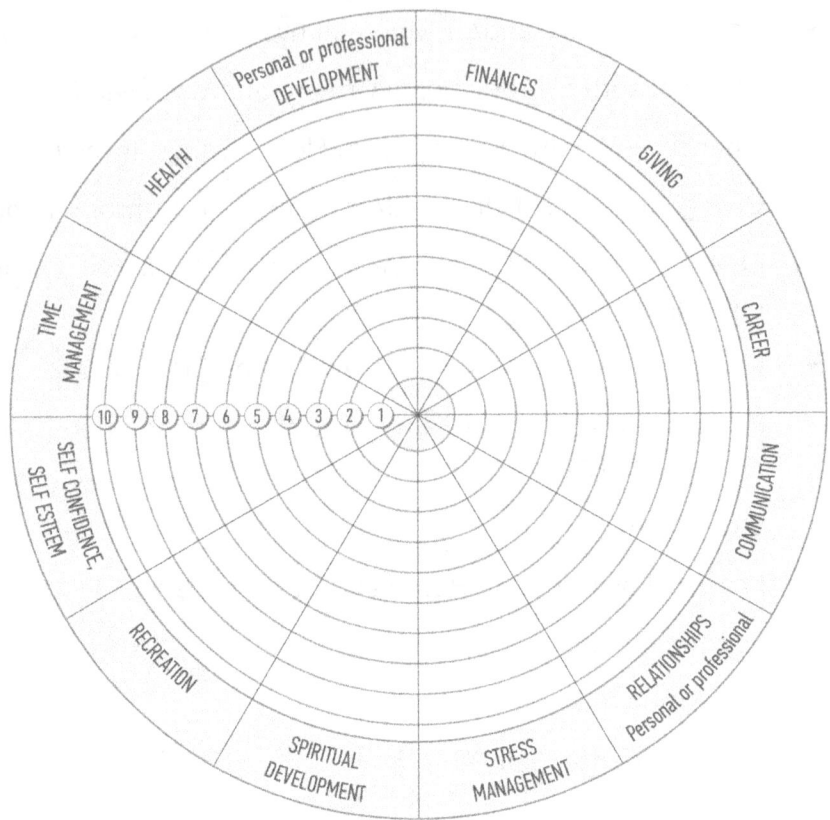

Once you have created your *Lifestyle Circle*, you then answer the question "How satisfied am I in this area right now?" Give a number from 1-10 to that level of satisfaction. One would be low and located towards the centre of the circle and ten would be high, at the outer edge.

There are two important distinctions in the question: The first is "How satisfied **am I**?" which is a subjective assessment. It is not about how your family, colleagues or neighbours see you, and it is not about success. It is about personal satisfaction. The second distinction is "**_right now_**".

This *Lifestyle Circle* is a snapshot of your life at this very moment. It is not about what you had or even where you would like to be. It's about where you are at right now. This is an exercise that you can repeat on a regular basis and you will probably find that your answers will continually change as your circumstances change.

This exercise is not about finding the ultimate truth, just a guide with how you feel in this moment.

Once you have scored each section, it's time to connect the dots. Draw a line across the sections so that it connects. If your life is well balanced this will show up as a circle. However, if your life is out of balance this can be a very strange shape.

The Full Circle

See the example of how your *Lifestyle Circle* could look when you have indicated where you fall within each of the listed categories:

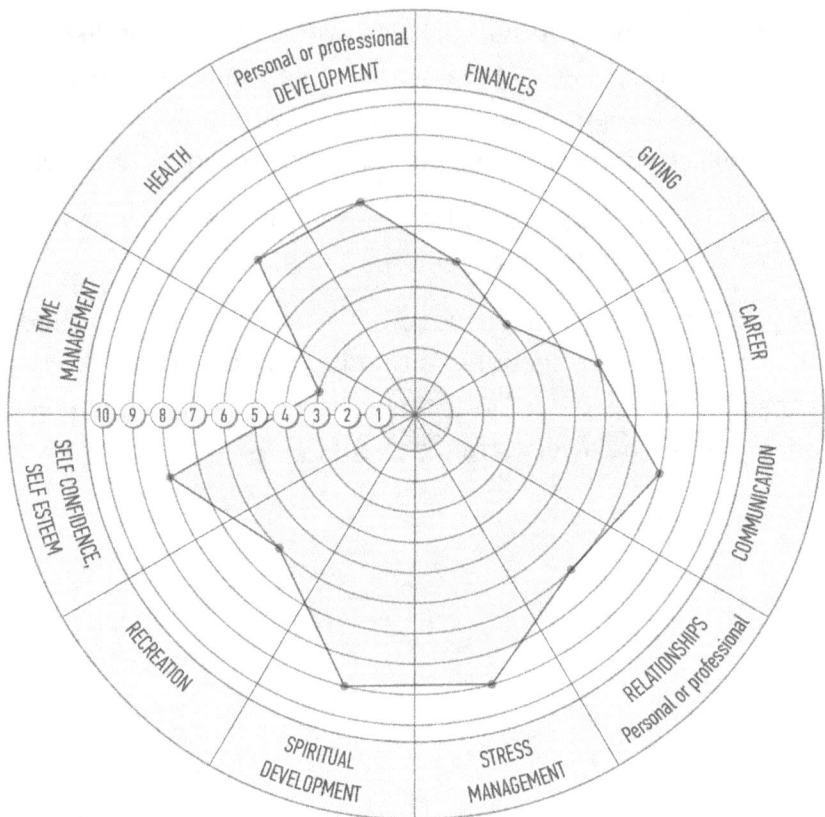

Stand back, take a look. What do you notice? Don't worry if it looks like a terribly wonky and odd circle that will have great difficulty turning. What you will have is something that shows you how to define your own balance circle, this being a reflection of how you perceive different areas of your life at this moment. In this way you will see where you may need change in your life if you are looking to have a more balanced life. Then you are able to look at ways of making those changes which will ultimately lead to a happier healthier lifestyle.

About the Author

Paulette Archer uses her natural gifts and extensive training to help women in her role as a *Women's Empowerment Leader*. Through her extensive training as a Life Coach, Neuro-Linguistic Programming Practitioner, Registered Nurse and Telephone Crisis Counsellor, and with her personal experiences, Paulette inspires women in transition, women who are lost, and women who have become disempowered due to circumstances beyond their control, to find their life's purpose.

After twenty-seven years of unhappiness in a troubled relationship, Paulette needed to heal and find new aspirations. She struggled for years in search of her true purpose only to recognise that it was to assist others in realising their purpose and dreams, and to find their own sense of self. With her new focus, she helps women work toward awareness, clarity, empowerment and purpose.

With Paulette's down-to-earth sense of compassion, her direct 'tell it like it is' approach, and her passion for life, she is able to deliver invaluable one-on-one coaching and mentoring to women who are desperate to make changes in their lives. Her gift is in her ability to handle difficult situations and working with women who are struggling. She educates her clients to use the tools she's created for personal development in healing themselves and discovering the value of self-love, taking tremendous joy in seeing a client become aware or reach an "ah-ha!" moment of clarity when everything falls into place and her entire being is transformed.

"My mission is ultimately, to have every woman on this planet empowered to choose and live the life they desire," says Paulette. "I will do everything in my power to make this happen for each and every person in my life. Take what you can from your life lessons and learn from them, because what you thought was the worst that could happen, may be what helps you grow stronger and more successful than you had possibly thought. If I can help women who have hit rock bottom and lost their purpose regain it again, I will have succeeded in my mission."

Paulette works with her clients to affect extraordinary change in their lives. With her assistance, they become empowered, learn to take full responsibility for their lives and find their true purpose. She believes that everything happens for a reason and if people can learn and grow from their experiences, they can turn a 'bad experience' into a powerfully transformative moment in their lives. She is there to help you find your feet, claim your power and regain your life.

> *"Everything happens for a reason: Trials should cause growth and wisdom rather than fear and despair."*
> **— Paulette Archer**

www.ingramcontent.com/pod-product-compliance
Lightning Source LLC
Chambersburg PA
CBHW070420010526
44118CB00014B/1837